The Art of Tactics

36 Strategies for Navigating Life and Business

B. Archer

London 2024

Preface

Navigating the complexities of daily life in the hustle and bustle of modern society often feels like a strategic battle. Each day, from the boardroom to personal relationships, presents new challenges that require effort, wisdom, and cunning. Inspired by ancient Chinese military tactics, this pocketbook offers a collection of 36 strategies reinterpreted for contemporary use.

These strategies, rooted in centuries-old wisdom, provide timeless guidance for overcoming obstacles, seizing opportunities, and achieving success. Whether you are managing a team, negotiating a deal, or simply trying to balance the demands of everyday life, these strategies will equip you with practical tools to approach situations with a strategic mindset.

As you read through each strategy, consider how it applies to your personal and professional circumstances. Adapt the insights to suit your unique challenges and watch as these ancient principles help you navigate the modern world more efficiently and effectively.

Embrace the wisdom of the ages and let these 36 strategies become your guide to mastering the art of living in today's fast-paced society.

Preface 3

Introduction 11

    Overview of the 36 Strategies 11

    Historical Context and Modern Relevance 12

    How to Use This Book 15

Strategy 1: Fool the Emperor to Cross the Sea 18

    Applications in Negotiation and Diplomacy . 18

Strategy 2: Besiege Wei to Rescue Zhao 22

    Applications in Business and Competitive Positioning 22

Strategy 3: Kill With a Borrowed Sword 26

    Applications in Business and Competitive Positioning 26

Strategy 4: Await the Exhausted Enemy at Your Ease 31

    Applications in Business and Competitive Positioning 31

Strategy 5: Loot a Burning House 35

    Applications in Business and Competitive Positioning 35

Strategy 6: Clamour in the East, Attack in the West 39

Applications in Business and Competitive Positioning 39

Strategy 7: Create Something from Nothing..43

Applications in Business and Competitive Positioning 43

Strategy 8: Openly Repair the Walkway, Secretly March to Chencang 47

Applications in Business and Competitive Positioning 47

Strategy 9: Observe the Fire on the Opposite Shore..51

Applications in Business and Competitive Positioning 51

Strategy 10: Hide Your Dagger Behind a Smile 56

Applications in Business and Competitive Positioning 56

Strategy 11: Sacrifice the Plum Tree in Place of the Peach 61

Applications in Business and Competitive Positioning 61

Strategy 12: Seize the Opportunity to Lead a Sheep Away..66

Applications in Business and Competitive Positioning 66

Strategy 13: Beat the Grass to Startle the Snake 71

    Applications in Business and Competitive Positioning 71

Strategy 14: Borrow a Corpse to Raise the Spirit 76

    Applications in Business and Competitive Positioning 76

Strategy 15: Lure the Tiger Down the Mountain 80

    Applications in Business and Competitive Positioning 80

Strategy 16: To Catch Something, First Let It Go 85

    Applications in Business and Competitive Positioning 85

Strategy 17: Toss out a Brick to Attract Jade. 90

    Applications in Business and Competitive Positioning 90

Strategy 18: To Catch the Bandits, First Capture Their Leader 95

    Applications in Business and Competitive Positioning 95

Strategy 19: Steal the Firewood from Under the Pot 100

    Applications in Business and Competitive Positioning 100

Strategy 20: Trouble the Water to Catch the Fish 104

    Applications in Business and Competitive Positioning 104

Strategy 21: Shed Your Skin Like the Golden Cicada 108

    Applications in Business and Competitive Positioning 108

Strategy 22: Shut the Door to Catch the Thief 113

    Applications in Business and Competitive Positioning 113

Strategy 23: Befriend a Distant Enemy to Attack One Nearby 117

    Applications in Business and Competitive Positioning 117

Strategy 24: Borrow the Road to Conquer Guo 122

    Applications in Business and Competitive Positioning 122

Strategy 25: Replace the Beams with Rotten Timbers 127

    Applications in Business and Competitive Positioning 127

Strategy 26: Point at the Mulberry but Curse the Locust Tree 131

    Applications in Business and Competitive Positioning 131

Strategy 27: Feign Madness, But Keep Your Balance 136

    Applications in Business and Competitive Positioning 136

Strategy 28: Lure Your Enemy onto the Roof, Then Take Away the Ladder 141

    Applications in Business and Competitive Positioning 141

Strategy 29: Tie Silk Blossoms to the Dead Tree 146

    Applications in Business and Competitive Positioning 146

Strategy 30: Exchange the Role of Guest for That of Host 151

    Applications in Business and Competitive Positioning 151

Strategy 31: The Strategy of Beautiful Women 156

    Applications in Business and Competitive Positioning 156

Strategy 32: The Strategy of Open City Gates 161

Applications in Business and Competitive Positioning 161

Strategy 33: The Strategy of Sowing Discord 166

Applications in Business and Competitive Positioning 166

Strategy 34: The Strategy of Injuring Yourself 171

Applications in Business and Competitive Positioning 171

Strategy 35: The Strategy of Combining Tactics 176

Applications in Business and Competitive Positioning 176

Strategy 36: If All Else Fails, Retreat 181

Applications in Business and Competitive Positioning 181

Conclusion 186

References 190

Introduction

Overview of the 36 Strategies

The "36 Strategies" is an ancient collection of Chinese tactics and strategies that offer insights into handling various warfare, politics, and interpersonal relations situations. These strategies, developed over centuries, are often attributed to the wisdom of military leaders and strategists from ancient China. Each strategy succinctly expresses a tactical principle, which can be applied to military situations and modern business, leadership, negotiation, and personal development.

The strategies are divided into six categories, each containing six strategies:

Winning Strategies:

These are proactive approaches to achieving victory in competitive situations. They emphasise surprise, deception, and leveraging strengths against opponents' weaknesses.

Examples:

"Fool the Emperor to Cross the Sea," "Besiege Wei to Rescue Zhao."

Enemy Dealing Strategies:

These strategies create advantageous situations by understanding and manipulating the opponent's behaviours or environment.

Examples:

"Kill with a Borrowed Sword," "Await the Exhausted Enemy at Your Ease."

Attacking Strategies:

This set includes tactics for aggressive manoeuvres and taking initiative. They often involve direct or indirect confrontation.

Examples:

"Clamour in the East, Attack in the West," "Loot a Burning House."

Confusion Strategies:

These strategies confuse, mislead, or disorient the opponent, making them easier to control or defeat.

Examples:

"Create Something from Nothing," "Observe the Fire on the Opposite Shore."

Gaining Ground Strategies emphasise gaining a tactical advantage, often through manipulation or exploiting opportunities.

Examples:

"Hide Your Dagger Behind a Smile," "Sacrifice the Plum Tree in Place of the Peach."

Desperate Strategies:

These are often last-resort strategies when facing overwhelming odds or when other methods have failed.

Examples:

"Exchange the Role of Guest for That of Host," "If All Else Fails, Retreat."

Each strategy provides a tactical lesson and conveys a deeper understanding of human nature, decision-making, and strategic thinking. This collection remains relevant today, offering valuable insights for navigating modern challenges in life and business. The strategies teach the importance of flexibility, observation, deception, and adaptation, making them timeless tools for anyone seeking to understand and master the art of strategy in modern business, leadership, negotiation, and personal development.

Historical Context and Modern Relevance

Historical Context

The "36 Strategies" is rooted in the rich tapestry of Chinese military history and philosophy, dating back to the Warring States period (475–221 BCE) and later eras. Although these strategies' precise origins and authorship are debated, they are commonly associated with the tactical wisdom of renowned strategists like Sun Tzu, author of "The Art of War," and other military leaders. The strategies encapsulate the essence of ancient Chinese strategic thought, which blends philosophical principles from Confucianism, Taoism, and Legalism with practical military tactics.

In ancient China, these strategies were often employed in warfare, statecraft, and diplomacy, where cunning, psychological insight and strategic deception played crucial roles in achieving success. They were used not only on the battlefield but also in court politics, business, and interpersonal relationships, reflecting a comprehensive approach to strategy where the lines between different domains were often blurred.

Modern Relevance

Despite their ancient origins, the '36 Strategies' remain highly relevant today. Their enduring appeal lies in their universal applicability to various contexts beyond traditional warfare, including business, leadership, negotiations, and personal development. Here's why these strategies remain pertinent today:

Strategic Thinking:

The strategies foster a mindset emphasising planning, anticipation, and adaptation. In a rapidly changing world, thinking strategically is crucial for navigating business, politics, and personal life complexities.

Psychological Insight:

Many strategies focus on understanding and influencing human behaviours. This can translate into effective leadership, marketing, negotiation, and conflict-resolution skills in contemporary settings.

Adaptability:
These strategies' flexibility allows them to adapt to various situations, whether outmanoeuvring a competitor in business, resolving conflicts, or managing crises. This adaptability makes them valuable tools in diverse fields, reinforcing their relevance in various situations.

Ethical Considerations:
The strategies also encourage reflection on ethical boundaries in strategy and tactics. While some strategies might seem manipulative, their study can lead to a deeper understanding of moral decision-making in complex situations, making you more morally conscious and responsible in your strategic endeavours.

Cross-Cultural Application:
Understanding diverse strategic perspectives becomes essential as globalisation increases, providing a reassuring and confidence-boosting guide for navigating modern challenges. The "36 Strategies" offer insights into non-Western strategic thinking, enriching global strategic discourse.

The "36 Strategies" provide a timeless framework for thinking about strategy that applies to modern leadership, business, and personal growth challenges. By studying these ancient principles, individuals and organisations can better understand strategic dynamics and enhance their ability to achieve desired outcomes in an increasingly interconnected and competitive world.

How to Use This Book

The Art of Tactics:

36 Strategies for Navigating Life and Business is designed as a practical guide to understanding and applying ancient strategic principles in today's complex and dynamic environments. Whether you are a business leader, entrepreneur, student, or someone interested in personal development, this book offers valuable insights into strategic thinking and decision-making.

1. Explore Each Strategy Individually

Each chapter is dedicated to one of the 36 strategies, explaining its historical context, core principles, and practical applications. You can read through the strategies in order or selectively choose those that resonate most with your current challenges or interests.

Historical Context:
Understand the origins and traditional use of each strategy.
Core Principles:
Grasp the fundamental ideas and tactical wisdom encapsulated in the strategy.
Practical Applications:
Discover how these ancient strategies can be applied to modern business, leadership, and personal scenarios. By understanding each strategy's practical applications, you will be equipped and confident to use them in your life and business, enhancing your strategic thinking and decision-making.

2. Reflect on Case Studies and Examples

The book includes real-world case studies and examples illustrating how each strategy has been successfully applied in contemporary settings. These examples range from corporate strategies and political manoeuvres to personal development tactics. Reflecting on these cases can help you see the practical relevance of each approach and inspire you to think about how to implement them in your context.

3. Practice Strategic Thinking

Each chapter ends with reflective questions and exercises designed to encourage strategic thinking. These prompts help you:

Analyse Situations:

Develop your ability to assess complex situations from a strategic perspective.

Formulate Strategies:

Practice crafting your strategies based on the principles discussed.

Evaluate Outcomes:

Reflect on strategic decisions' potential and actual outcomes.

4. Integrate Strategies into Daily Life

The "36 Strategies" are theoretical concepts and actionable tactics that can be integrated into daily decision-making. Whether dealing with business negotiations, managing teams, navigating personal relationships, or planning long-term goals, these strategies provide a versatile toolkit for enhancing your strategic capabilities.

5. Adapt and Innovate

While the book provides traditional interpretations and applications, adapting these strategies to fit contemporary contexts and your unique circumstances is essential. Innovation and creativity in applying these strategies can lead to unexpected insights and solutions.

6. Ethical Considerations

While exploring these strategies, consider the ethical implications of your actions. Some methods may involve deception or manipulation; balancing effectiveness with integrity and fairness is crucial. Use this book to enhance your strategic acumen while upholding ethical standards.

7. Further Exploration

The book concludes with recommendations for further reading and resources, allowing you to delve deeper into specific areas of interest, including strategic management, psychology, and historical case studies.

By engaging with this book, you will learn about the 36 ancient strategies and develop a more nuanced and practical approach to navigating modern life and business complexities. Use this guide as a springboard to refine your strategic thinking, improve decision-making, and achieve tremendous success in various aspects of your life.

Strategy 1: Fool the Emperor to Cross the Sea

Core Concept: Deception in Plain Sight

The strategy "Fool the Emperor to Cross the Sea" revolves around achieving a goal through deception so open and evident that it is not perceived as a deception. This tactic leverages the human tendency to overlook the obvious, especially when it appears too blatant to be a trick. By creating a distraction or presenting a misleading narrative, one can conceal their true intentions and accomplish objectives unnoticed.

Applications in Negotiation and Diplomacy

1. Negotiation Context:

The Art of the Decoy Offer

In negotiations, parties often employ various tactics to gain favourable terms. The "decoy offer" practically applies the "Fool the Emperor to Cross the Sea" strategy. In this context, a negotiator presents an offer deliberately designed to be less attractive or unacceptable, knowing it will likely be rejected. The fundamental objective is to divert attention away from the main offer, which is more favourable to them and comes later in the negotiation.

Example:

Salary Negotiation

Imagine a job candidate negotiating a salary with a potential employer. The candidate may initially propose an unusually high salary or request extensive benefits, which they do not expect to be accepted. The employer, seeing this as unreasonable, may counter with a lower offer closer to the candidate's desires. The initial high offer serves as a decoy, making the employer feel they have gained a concession while the candidate achieves their goal.

2. Diplomatic Context:

The Conspicuous Initiative

In diplomacy, nations often use strategic moves to influence international relations or negotiations. A country might undertake an action that seems straightforward or transparent but is designed to achieve a hidden agenda.

Example:

Environmental Agreements

A country may prominently propose an environmental initiative that appears altruistic and progressive, such as committing to stringent carbon emission reductions. However, the underlying intention might be to gain leverage in trade negotiations or to position itself as a global leader on climate issues, thereby increasing its influence in international bodies like the United Nations. The overt environmental stance serves as a smokescreen, diverting attention from the country's broader strategic objectives, such as securing economic concessions or building alliances.

Fundamental Principles and Ethical Considerations

Key Principles:

Simplicity and Obviousness:

The deception must be open and straightforward, making it appear that no hidden motives exist.

Timing and Execution:

The success of this strategy often depends on timing and the ability to execute the decoy convincingly.

Perception Management:

Effective use of this strategy requires careful management of how others perceive the situation.

Ethical Considerations:

Trust and Integrity:

While this strategy can be effective, it must be used cautiously to avoid damaging trust or relationships. Overuse or misuse can lead to perceptions of dishonesty and can harm one's reputation in the long term.

Transparency:

Balancing strategic deception and transparency is crucial in diplomacy and negotiation. Parties must ensure that deception does not cross ethical boundaries or legal norms.

By understanding and judiciously applying the "Fool the Emperor to Cross the Sea" strategy, individuals and organisations can navigate complex negotiations and diplomatic situations more effectively, achieving their goals while maintaining necessary ethical standards.

Strategy 2: Besiege Wei to Rescue Zhao

Core Concept: Indirect Strategies for Conflict Resolution

The strategy "Besiege Wei to Rescue Zhao" originates from an ancient Chinese military tactic in which an army attacked a secondary or weaker target instead of the main force, which directly compelled the main force to retreat or divert its focus. This indirect approach aims to resolve conflicts by altering the balance of power or shifting focus, thereby achieving the desired outcome without confrontation.

Applications in Business and Competitive Positioning

1. Indirect Strategies for Conflict Resolution

Confrontation with competitors and stakeholders or internal conflicts can often be costly and damaging to a business. Indirect strategies, such as "Besiege Wei to Rescue Zhao," can offer more subtle and effective ways to resolve conflicts.

Example:

Internal Conflict Resolution

Imagine a company facing internal conflict over resource allocation between departments A and B. Instead of directly intervening in the conflict;

management decides to invest in training and development for department C. This move indirectly supports the needs of both A and B by increasing overall productivity and resource efficiency. It alleviates the conflict by addressing underlying issues without directly engaging in the dispute.

Example:

Negotiation Tactics

In a negotiation setting, if a company struggles with a client over contract terms, it might work on strengthening its relationships with other vital clients or stakeholders instead of confronting the issue head-on. By showcasing their strong market position and client base, they indirectly pressure the difficult client to reconsider their stance, leading to a more favourable negotiation outcome.

2. Business and Competitive Positioning

In competitive business environments, companies often use indirect strategies to position themselves advantageously without engaging in direct competition, which can be costly and risky.

Example:

Product Positioning and Market Entry

A company planning to enter a new market where a competitor has a strong presence might choose not to compete directly in the competitor's most vital area. Instead, it could focus on a niche or underserved market segment. Excelling in this niche would build a loyal customer base and strengthen its position. This strategy indirectly pressures the competitor, who may adjust their focus or resources to respond, weakening their position in their core area.

Example:

Strategic Alliances

Rather than engaging in a direct market share battle, a company might form strategic alliances or partnerships with other businesses, such as suppliers or smaller firms, to enhance its product offerings or distribution channels. This can indirectly weaken the competitor's influence and market share as the company grows stronger through these alliances and increased market presence.

Fundamental Principles and Ethical Considerations

Key Principles:

Focus on Leverage Points:

Identify weaker or less defended areas that, when targeted, can shift the overall balance of power.

Resource Efficiency:

Use resources more efficiently by avoiding confrontation, which can be resource-intensive.

Flexibility and Adaptability:

Be adaptable and willing to change tactics based on the evolving situation and responses from competitors or stakeholders.

Ethical Considerations:

Fair Competition:

While indirect strategies can be effective, it is crucial to ensure they are used fairly and ethically to avoid manipulation or exploitation.

Transparency and Communication:

Maintain clear communication with stakeholders to ensure indirect strategies do not cause misunderstandings or distrust.

By applying the "Besiege Wei to Rescue Zhao" strategy in business, companies can resolve conflicts and improve their competitive positioning to conserve resources and minimise confrontation. This approach helps maintain a positive corporate image and fosters a more strategic and thoughtful way of handling challenges.

Strategy 3: Kill With a Borrowed Sword

Core Concept: Utilizing External Resources and Alliances

The strategy "Kill with a Borrowed Sword" involves achieving one's objectives by using the resources, influence, or efforts of others. This approach allows one to accomplish goals without expending resources, taking risks, or directly engaging in conflict. It is about leveraging external assets or alliances to gain an advantage.

Applications in Business and Competitive Positioning

1. Utilizing External Resources and Alliances

In the business world, leveraging external resources and alliances can be a powerful strategy for achieving objectives such as entering new markets, developing new products, or gaining a competitive edge.

Example:

Strategic Partnerships

A technology startup lacking the resources to develop a new product line might partner with a larger, more established company with the necessary technology and expertise. By collaborating, the startup can bring the new product to market faster and more efficiently than if it were to go alone. The more considerable company benefits by accessing the startup's innovative ideas or niche market segment. This "borrowing" of resources allows both companies to achieve goals that might have been difficult independently.

Example:

Brand Licensing

In another scenario, a company looking to expand its product offerings without the cost of developing new products from scratch might license a well-known brand. For instance, a food manufacturer could license a popular children's cartoon character to feature on its packaging, leveraging its established popularity to boost sales and market presence. The company effectively "borrows" the cartoon character's brand equity to enhance its product's appeal.

2. Leveraging Outsourcing and Partnerships

Outsourcing and strategic partnerships are modern business practices that align closely with "killing with a borrowed sword." Companies can focus on their core competencies by relying on external entities while achieving more with less direct investment.

Example:

Outsourcing Non-Core Functions

A company might outsource its IT services, customer support, or manufacturing processes to specialised firms. This allows the company to maintain a lean operation, reduce costs, and focus on product innovation and marketing activities. The outsourcing partner brings expertise and scale, providing services more efficiently than the company could in-house.

Example:

Joint Ventures

In cases where market entry barriers are high, a company may form a joint venture with a local firm. For instance, a Western automotive company might partner with a local manufacturer in an emerging market. This partnership allows the foreign company to leverage the local partner's market knowledge, regulatory understanding, and distribution networks. In contrast, the local company benefits from the foreign partner's technology and brand reputation.

Fundamental Principles and Ethical Considerations

Key Principles:

Maximize Efficiency:

Use external resources to achieve goals more efficiently than internal ones alone.

Risk Mitigation:

By leveraging external parties, companies can share or transfer risk, reducing their exposure.

Strategic Focus:

Concentrate on core competencies while using external alliances to handle other critical but non-core activities.

Ethical Considerations:

Transparency and Fairness:

Ensure that all parties in the alliance or outsourcing arrangement benefit pretty and transparently.

Quality and Control:

Maintain control over quality and brand integrity, even when outsourced activities or partners are involved.

Long-term Relationships:

Cultivate solid and long-term relationships with partners to build trust and reliability.

The "Kill with a Borrowed Sword" strategy highlights the importance of leveraging external resources and alliances in modern business. By strategically outsourcing, partnering, or collaborating, companies can achieve significant objectives, enhance their competitive positioning, and navigate complex market environments more effectively. This approach optimises resource use and fosters innovation and growth through collaborative efforts.

Strategy 4: Await the Exhausted Enemy at Your Ease

Core Concept: Patience as a Strategic Advantage

The strategy "Await the Exhausted Enemy at Your Ease" emphasises the importance of patience and timing in achieving strategic advantage. The core idea is to conserve one's resources and strength while allowing an opponent to deplete their energy, morale, or resources. Once the opponent is weakened, a well-timed action can decisively turn the situation in one's favour. This strategy highlights the value of readiness, patience, and strategic restraint.

Applications in Business and Competitive Positioning

1. Patience as a Strategic Advantage

Patience can be a critical strategic asset in business, especially in competitive markets. Companies that can wait for the right moment to act, rather than rushing into decisions, can often achieve better outcomes.

Example:

Market Entry Timing

A company looking to enter a new market might wait for existing competitors to exhaust their resources in aggressive marketing campaigns or expansion efforts. By observing how the market responds and learning from competitors' mistakes, the company can enter the market more strategically, with a better understanding of customer needs and market dynamics. This allows the company to position itself more effectively and capture market share without the same level of initial expenditure.

Example:

Product Launch Strategies

In technology and consumer goods, companies often rush to launch new products to stay ahead of competitors. However, a company that waits until the initial excitement dies down can benefit from improved product development and market readiness. By launching a refined product with better features or addressing issues seen in competitors' offerings, the company can attract customers who are looking for a reliable and well-tested product, thereby gaining a competitive edge.

2. Stress Management and Decision Timing

Managing stress and timing decisions are critical aspects of strategic thinking in both personal and professional settings. Making decisions under pressure or without adequate preparation can lead to suboptimal outcomes.

Example:

Stress Management in Leadership

Leaders often face pressure to make quick decisions, especially during crises. However, those who can manage their stress and wait until they understand the situation are more likely to make better decisions. For instance, a company might face pressure to cut costs rapidly during economic downturns. A patient leader might instead opt for a thorough review of operations to find sustainable cost-saving measures rather than making hasty layoffs or cuts that could harm long-term prospects.

Example:

Timing in Negotiations

In negotiations, patience can be a powerful tool. A negotiator who can wait for the other party to show signs of desperation or urgency is often in a stronger position. By understanding the timing of the counterpart's needs or deadlines, a negotiator can better gauge when to make concessions or stand firm, potentially securing more favourable terms.

Fundamental Principles and Ethical Considerations

Key Principles:

Conserve Resources:

Focus on maintaining and optimising your resources, energy, and strategic assets while waiting for the optimal time to act.

Observe and Learn:

Use the waiting period to gather intelligence, observe competitors or opponents, and learn from their actions and mistakes.

Strategic Patience:

Develop the discipline to wait for the right moment to make a move rather than acting impulsively.

Ethical Considerations:

Avoid Exploitation:

While patience can be strategic, avoiding exploiting others' vulnerabilities unethically is vital.

Transparency and Communication:

In situations involving team members or stakeholders, maintaining clear communication about why decisions are being delayed can help manage expectations and maintain trust.

The strategy "Await the Exhausted Enemy at Your Ease" teaches the value of patience and timing in strategy. Whether in business, leadership, or personal endeavours, the ability to wait for the right moment can lead to more effective decisions and better outcomes, ultimately providing a strategic advantage in competitive or challenging situations.

Strategy 5: Loot a Burning House

Core Concept: Seizing Opportunities in Crisis

The strategy "Loot a Burning House" involves taking advantage of opportunities that arise from the chaos or misfortune of others. This tactic is about recognising and seizing the chance to benefit from a situation where others are in disarray or facing crises. By acting swiftly and strategically during these turbulent times, one can gain a significant advantage or achieve goals that might otherwise be difficult.

Applications in Business and Competitive Positioning

1. Seizing Opportunities in Crisis

Crises can create unique opportunities, but only for those who are prepared to act decisively and strategically. Identifying and capitalizing on these opportunities can lead to significant gains, highlighting the importance of readiness in crisis response.

Example:

Market Disruption

When a significant competitor faces a public relations crisis or operational failure, other companies in the industry might seize this opportunity to capture market share. For instance, if a leading tech company experiences a massive product recall, its competitors can step in with their offerings, potentially gaining dissatisfied customers or those seeking alternatives.

Example:

Economic Downturns

Some businesses find opportunities during economic recessions, whereas others see only challenges. For example, a company might acquire struggling but valuable assets, such as intellectual property or talent, at a lower cost. Similarly, startups might find it easier to recruit top talent from downsizing companies, gaining skilled employees who are available due to the crisis.

2. Crisis Management and Turnaround Strategies

Effective crisis management is not just about managing the immediate situation but also about leveraging the opportunities that arise from it. Turnaround strategies can turn a crisis into an opportunity for improvement and growth, underscoring the strategic importance of crisis management.

Example:

Turnaround Management

A company in financial trouble might use a crisis as an impetus for a significant turnaround. For example, a retail chain facing declining sales and profitability could use the crisis as a catalyst to completely overhaul its business model, focusing on e-commerce and digital transformation. The crisis forces the company to adapt and innovate, potentially leading to a more resilient and competitive business.

Example:

Strategic Acquisitions

When a sector is hit by a crisis, such as a pandemic or regulatory changes, companies with strong financial positions might acquire struggling competitors or related businesses at reduced prices. This can allow the acquirer to expand its market share, diversify its offerings, or enter new markets at a lower cost, setting the stage for future growth once the crisis subsides.

Fundamental Principles and Ethical Considerations

Key Principles:

Quick Action:

It is crucial to act swiftly in response to emerging opportunities. Crises create time-sensitive opportunities that require immediate attention.

Assessment of Risk and Reward:

Carefully assess the risks of taking advantage of a crisis, ensuring the potential rewards outweigh the risks.

Readiness:

Prepare for potential crises with strategies and resources to capitalise on opportunities quickly.

Ethical Considerations:

Fairness and Responsibility:

Ensure that actions taken during a crisis do not unethically exploit others' misfortunes. Strive for responsible and fair practices.

Long-Term Impact:

Consider the long-term implications of your actions. Taking advantage of a crisis should align with your overall values and business strategy, maintaining a positive reputation and relationships.

The strategy "Loot a Burning House" emphasises the importance of recognising and seizing opportunities that arise during times of crisis or upheaval. Individuals and organisations can achieve significant advantages and drive growth by strategically leveraging these situations. However, balancing opportunism with ethical considerations and long-term impact is essential to ensure sustainable success and maintain a positive reputation.

Strategy 6: Clamour in the East, Attack in the West

Core Concept: Misdirection and Surprise

The strategy "Clamour in the East, Attack in the West" involves creating a diversion or distraction in one area to mislead opponents while executing a decisive action in a different, less-expected area. This approach uses misdirection to divert attention and resources, making the true objective more achievable and successful. It emphasises the power of surprise and the effectiveness of strategic planning to outmanoeuvre competitors.

Applications in Business and Competitive Positioning

1. Misdirection and Surprise

Creating diversions and leveraging surprise can be effective tactics for gaining a competitive advantage or achieving strategic goals.

Example:

Marketing Campaigns

A company might launch a high-profile, attention-grabbing marketing campaign to generate buzz and draw public attention. While competitors are focused on countering this campaign, the company can simultaneously introduce a new product or service in a different segment or market. The initial clamour diverts competitors' focus from the latest launch, maximising its impact and market reception.

Example:

Strategic Product Launches

In a competitive industry, a company may create a false sense of urgency or hype around an upcoming product to distract competitors. For example, they might release a teaser for a less critical product to their business strategy while quietly preparing to release a more impactful innovation. When the actual game-changing product is launched, it surprises the market and competitors, leveraging the initial misdirection for maximum effect.

2. Strategic Planning and Diversification

Effective strategic planning involves not only executing immediate tactics but also thinking ahead about how to diversify and position oneself advantageously.

Example:

Business Expansion

A company looking to enter a new market might first create a strong presence in an adjacent or related market. This initial presence can attract attention and create a perception of dominance. Meanwhile, the company can work on entering the target market, where its actual strategy and value proposition are fully developed and ready. This method can reduce the direct competition and scrutiny in the new market, allowing for a smoother entry.

Example:

Competitive Manoeuvring

In a highly competitive sector, a business might use misdirection by focusing its public relations efforts on a new, less critical initiative while quietly executing a significant operational improvement or acquisition. Competitors' focus on the diversion allows the company to implement its real strategy with less interference, leading to a stronger competitive position once the dust settles.

Fundamental Principles and Ethical Considerations

Key Principles:

Effective Use of Resources:

Use resources to create meaningful diversions or distractions that mislead competitors or opponents.

Strategic Timing:

Plan the diversion's timing and action to maximise the surprise element.

Coordination and Execution:

Ensure that the diversion and the primary strategy are well-coordinated and executed seamlessly to avoid failure or exposure.

Ethical Considerations:

Transparency and Integrity:

While misdirection can be a legitimate tactic, it should not involve deceptive practices that compromise ethical standards or harm stakeholders.

Long-Term Relationships:

Consider how these strategies impact long-term relationships with customers, partners, and other stakeholders. Misdirection should not damage trust or reputation.

The strategy "Clamour in the East, Attack in the West" underscores the importance of misdirection and surprise in achieving strategic goals. Businesses and individuals can gain a competitive edge and effectively manage their resources by creating distractions and executing well-planned actions in less-expected areas. Balancing these tactics with ethical considerations ensures that strategic manoeuvres lead to sustainable success and maintain positive relationships.

Strategy 7: Create Something from Nothing

Core Concept: Innovation and Creativity

The strategy "Create Something from Nothing" emphasises the ability to generate value, ideas, or products from seemingly barren or limited resources. This approach involves leveraging creativity and resourcefulness to innovate and create opportunities where none initially exist. It's about transforming constraints and scarcity into advantages by thinking outside the box and using available resources in novel ways.

Applications in Business and Competitive Positioning

1. Innovation and Creativity

Innovating and thinking creatively can turn limited resources into significant opportunities in business. Companies and entrepreneurs must often create value from minimal resources or challenging conditions.

Example:

Bootstrapping Startups

Many successful startups begin with limited funding and resources. Entrepreneurs who bootstrap their startups (i.e., build their businesses using personal savings or small amounts of capital) often must get creative with their approach. For instance, a tech startup might develop a minimum viable product (MVP) using open-source software and inexpensive tools, focusing on solving a niche problem. They can attract early adopters and investors by leveraging creativity and innovation, eventually scaling their business.

Example:

Pivoting Business Models

When facing market challenges, companies can pivot their business models to create new value from existing resources. For instance, a restaurant struck by the COVID-19 pandemic might start offering meal kits and online cooking classes. They make a new revenue stream and adapt to changing customer needs by repurposing their kitchen space and leveraging their chefs' skills.

2. Building from Scarcity and Constraints

Constraints and scarcity often drive innovation, forcing individuals and organisations to find creative solutions and optimise their use of resources.

Example:

Resourceful Product Development

A company might face a shortage of critical raw materials due to supply chain disruptions. Instead of halting production, the company could innovate by developing a new product using alternative materials or redesigning existing products to be more resource-efficient. For example, during material shortages, some manufacturers have developed eco-friendly alternatives that address the shortage and appeal to environmentally conscious consumers.

Example:

Developing New Markets

Companies can create new opportunities in a saturated market by identifying and serving underserved niches or creating new categories. For instance, when the demand for traditional fitness equipment becomes crowded, a company might innovate by introducing wearable fitness technology that tracks unique health metrics or integrates with other digital health solutions. This approach leverages scarcity in traditional market space to create a new and valuable offering.

Fundamental Principles and Ethical Considerations

Key Principles:

Resource Optimization:

Use available resources creatively and efficiently to maximise their potential and create value.

Innovation Mindset:

Foster a culture of creativity and innovation that encourages experimenting with new ideas and approaches.

Adaptability:

Be willing to pivot and adapt strategies based on the existing constraints and opportunities.

Ethical Considerations:

Integrity and Transparency:

Ensure creative solutions and innovations are developed ethically and transparently, avoiding misleading practices or exploitation.

Sustainable Practices:

Consider the long-term impact of innovations on the environment and society, striving to develop sustainable and responsible solutions.

The "Create Something from Nothing" strategy highlights the power of innovation and creativity in overcoming constraints and scarcity. Individuals and organisations can achieve significant success and growth by transforming limitations into opportunities and leveraging available resources in novel ways. Embracing this approach fosters a proactive and resilient mindset and drives progress and adaptability in challenging environments.

Strategy 8: Openly Repair the Walkway, Secretly March to Chencang

Core Concept: Strategic Deception and Subterfuge

The strategy "Openly Repair the Walkway, Secretly March to Chencang" involves creating a deceptive or misleading public appearance while secretly pursuing a different, more strategic goal. This tactic relies on diverting attention and managing perceptions to mask true intentions and actions. By openly engaging in activities that appear benign or unrelated, one can secretly advance a more critical or strategic objective.

Applications in Business and Competitive Positioning

1. Strategic Deception and Subterfuge

In business, strategic deception can be used to mislead competitors or stakeholders while working towards meaningful goals. This tactic can help manage competitive dynamics and control the narrative.

Example:

Competitive Product Development

A technology company might publicly focus on developing a product that is not expected to disrupt the market significantly. Meanwhile, the company's genuine efforts are directed secretly toward a groundbreaking technology or product. By diverting competitors' attention and resources toward the less significant product, the company can ensure its major innovation is launched with minimal interference and maximum impact.

Example:

Market Entry Strategy

A company planning to enter a new market might initially establish a presence with low-profile activities that do not draw significant attention. For instance, it might start by offering consulting services or small-scale partnerships unrelated to its core business. While competitors and market observers are focused on these activities, the company secretly prepares a significant product launch or acquisition that will significantly impact the market.

2. R&D and Product Launch Tactics

Strategic deception can manage timing and expectations in research and development (R&D) and product launches, ensuring that critical innovations are introduced effectively.

Example:

Concealing R&D Focus

A company might publicly announce its focus on incremental improvements to existing products while its R&D teams work on a revolutionary new technology. By maintaining this facade, the company can avoid paying too much attention to its genuine innovation efforts, reducing the likelihood of competitors copying or accelerating their efforts in the same area. This allows the company to maintain a competitive edge and introduce its breakthrough technology with less direct competition.

Example:

Coordinated Product Launches

A company might use subterfuge during a product launch by creating multiple more minor announcements or teaser campaigns that distract from the main product. For example, a company could launch a series of minor updates or new features that generate buzz and speculation. At the same time, the actual high-impact product release is kept under wraps until the strategic moment. This approach maximises the impact of the main product launch and manages competitive responses.

Fundamental Principles and Ethical Considerations

Key Principles:

- **Controlled Information**:
- Manage the flow of information to ensure that competitors and stakeholders are not aware of the accurate strategic moves.
- **Effective Timing**:

- Time the revelation of the strategic objective carefully to maximise its impact and minimise competitive interference.
- **Coordination and Execution**:
- Ensure that the deceptive and strategic actions are well-coordinated and executed to achieve the desired outcomes.

Ethical Considerations:

- **Transparency and Trust**:
- While strategic deception can be a helpful tactic, it's essential to maintain transparency and trust with customers, partners, and stakeholders. Avoid misleading or deceptive practices that could damage long-term relationships or reputations.
- **Long-Term Impact**:
- Consider the potential long-term consequences of using deception. Ensure that the strategy aligns with ethical standards and does not compromise integrity.

The strategy "Openly Repair the Walkway, Secretly March to Chencang" demonstrates the effectiveness of strategic deception and fraud in achieving significant objectives. Businesses can advance their goals more effectively by managing public perceptions and creating misleading appearances. This approach requires careful planning and execution but can provide a substantial competitive advantage when applied ethically and responsibly.

Strategy 9: Observe the Fire on the Opposite Shore

Core Concept: Detachment and Objective Analysis

The "Observe the Fire on the Opposite Shore" strategy involves maintaining a detached and objective perspective while analysing others' situations, mainly in crisis or turmoil. By observing and understanding the difficulties and dynamics affecting others, one can gain valuable insights and leverage these observations to make informed decisions and strategies.

Applications in Business and Competitive Positioning

1. Detachment and Objective Analysis

Detachment and objective analysis in the business allows for better decision-making and strategic planning. This involves stepping back from immediate concerns to objectively assess external situations and trends that may impact one's strategies.

Example:

Industry Trends

A company might closely monitor and analyse trends in a related industry experiencing significant challenges or transformations. For instance, a firm in the renewable energy sector might observe regulatory changes and market disruptions in the traditional energy sector. By objectively analysing these developments, the company can anticipate shifts in demand, identify potential new opportunities, and adjust its strategy accordingly to capitalise on emerging trends.

Example:

Crisis Management

When a competitor faces a public relations crisis or operational failure, a business can observe and analyse the situation from a detached perspective. By understanding the competitor's challenges and responses, the company can develop strategies to position itself as a more attractive alternative or capitalise on the competitor's weakened state. This strategic observation allows the business to navigate the competitive landscape more effectively.

2. Competitive Intelligence Gathering

Observing competitors or industry trends provides crucial insights for competitive intelligence. This involves gathering and analysing information about competitors' strategies, strengths, weaknesses, and market behaviour to inform one's own strategic decisions.

Example:

Benchmarking and Analysis

A company might use competitive benchmarking, systematically observing and analysing competitors' performance metrics, product offerings, and customer feedback. This analysis can reveal gaps in the market, emerging trends, and potential areas for improvement or differentiation. For instance, by studying a competitor's recent product launch, a company can identify strengths and weaknesses, adapt its product development, and refine its marketing strategy.

Example:

Market and Consumer Insights

By observing shifts in consumer behaviour and preferences in related sectors, businesses can gather intelligence that informs their product development and marketing strategies. For instance, if consumer interest is rapidly shifting towards sustainable products, a company in the consumer goods sector might invest in sustainability initiatives and eco-friendly product lines to align with market demands and attract environmentally conscious customers.

Fundamental Principles and Ethical Considerations

Key Principles:

Objective Observation:

Maintain an impartial perspective when analysing external situations, focusing on facts and data rather than personal biases or emotions.

Comprehensive Analysis:

Gather and analyse a wide range of information to thoroughly understand external dynamics and their implications.

Strategic Adaptation:

Use insights from observation to adapt and refine strategies, ensuring that decisions are informed by relevant and accurate information.

Ethical Considerations:

Respect for Privacy:

Respect privacy and legal boundaries while gathering competitive intelligence. Avoid unethical practices such as espionage or unauthorised access to confidential information.

Transparency and Integrity:

Ensure that the strategies developed based on observations align with ethical standards and do not involve misleading or deceptive practices.

The "Observe the Fire on the Opposite Shore" strategy underscores the value of detachment and objective analysis in strategic decision-making. By observing and understanding the challenges and dynamics affecting others, businesses and individuals can make more informed decisions, adapt their strategies, and leverage competitive intelligence effectively. This approach facilitates strategic planning and positioning, helping to navigate complex, competitive environments and seize growth opportunities.

Strategy 10: Hide Your Dagger Behind a Smile

Core Concept: Charm and Strategic Manipulation

The "Hide Your Dagger Behind a Smile" strategy involves using charm and outward friendliness to mask underlying intentions or strategies. This tactic relies on creating a favourable impression or establishing trust while secretly pursuing strategic goals or leveraging opportunities. By presenting a friendly and accommodating demeanour, one can subtly influence situations to achieve desired outcomes without revealing true intentions.

Applications in Business and Competitive Positioning

1. Charm and Strategic Manipulation

In business, the ability to use charm and strategic manipulation can be an effective tool for achieving objectives and influencing others. This involves creating positive relationships and using social skills to advance personal or organisational goals.

Example:

Negotiation Tactics

One might use charm and diplomacy during negotiations to build rapport and create a cooperative atmosphere. A negotiator can gain the other party's trust and subtly guide the discussion towards favourable terms by being friendly and agreeable. For instance, a salesperson might use flattery and attentiveness to make a potential client feel valued while strategically positioning their product or service as the ideal solution.

Example:

Influencing Stakeholders

When seeking support for a new initiative or project, presenting oneself as approachable and considerate can help persuade stakeholders. A leader might use charm to foster strong relationships with key stakeholders, gaining their backing for a project. The leader's outward friendliness can mask the more aggressive strategies or objectives being pursued behind the scenes.

2. Networking and Persuasion Techniques

Effective networking and persuasion often involve projecting a positive image while subtly advancing one's interests. By mastering charm and persuasion, individuals can build valuable connections and influence outcomes in their favour.

Example:

Building Strategic Partnerships

In building strategic partnerships, using charm can help establish and strengthen relationships. For instance, when approaching potential partners, one might focus on creating a positive and engaging interaction, highlighting mutual benefits and demonstrating genuine interest. This approach can open doors to collaborative opportunities and favourable agreements while keeping the more aggressive aspects of the negotiation in the background.

Example:

Persuasive Communication

Employing charm and persuasive techniques can enhance the likelihood of acceptance when presenting new ideas or proposals. This might involve framing ideas that resonate with the audience's values and interests while subtly guiding them towards a particular viewpoint or decision. By combining charisma with well-crafted arguments, one can effectively influence others while masking underlying strategic goals.

Fundamental Principles and Ethical Considerations

Key Principles:

Authenticity and Trust:

Use charm and friendliness authentically to build genuine relationships and trust, which can enhance the effectiveness of strategic manipulation.

Strategic Discretion:

Maintain discretion about true intentions and strategies to achieve the desired outcomes without unnecessary conflict or resistance.

Skilful Persuasion:

Employ persuasive techniques ethically and professionally, ensuring that manipulative tactics are used responsibly and do not harm others.

Ethical Considerations:

Transparency and Honesty:

Ensure that charm and manipulation are not used to deceive or mislead in a way that could damage relationships or reputations. Aim for transparency in dealings where possible.

Respect and Integrity:

Use persuasion and charm to respect others' perspectives and interests. Avoid manipulative practices that undermine trust or ethical standards.

The "Hide Your Dagger Behind a Smile" strategy highlights the effectiveness of using charm and strategic manipulation to achieve goals while maintaining a cheerful and friendly exterior. Individuals and organisations can influence outcomes and advance their objectives by skillfully navigating social interactions and leveraging persuasive techniques. However, balancing these tactics with ethical considerations is crucial to ensure that strategies are implemented with integrity and respect for others.

Strategy 11: Sacrifice the Plum Tree in Place of the Peach

Core Concept: Strategic Sacrifice for Greater Gain

The strategy 'Sacrifice the Plum Tree in Place of the Peach' involves making a more minor, less critical sacrifice to achieve a more significant or strategic gain. This tactic recognises when letting go of something of lesser value is beneficial to secure an immense benefit or achieve a more critical objective. In the business context, this could mean reallocating resources, shifting focus, or making decisions that may initially seem disadvantageous but are intended to secure a more substantial benefit or advantage in the long run. It emphasises the importance of prioritising long-term gains over short-term losses.

Applications in Business and Competitive Positioning

1. Strategic Sacrifice for Greater Gain

In business, strategic sacrifices can involve reallocating resources, shifting focus, or making decisions that may initially seem disadvantageous but are intended to secure a more substantial benefit or advantage in the long run.

Example:

Product Line Adjustment

For instance, a technology firm might phase out an outdated product that no longer aligns with current market trends, redirecting those resources toward developing a new, innovative product with more significant potential. Another example could be a company discontinuing an un-profitable service, allowing them to focus on more lucrative business areas. This strategic sacrifice enables the company to concentrate on areas with higher growth prospects and competitive advantages.

Example:

Divesting Non-Core Assets

A business might sell or divest non-core assets or business units to streamline operations and enhance focus on its core competencies. For example, a conglomerate with diverse business interests might divest a subsidiary that does not align with its strategic vision. By making this sacrifice, the company can invest more effectively in its primary areas of strength and growth, leading to tremendous organisational success.

2. Cost-benefit analysis in Business Decisions

Conducting a cost-benefit analysis helps businesses evaluate the potential trade-offs and long-term impacts of making strategic sacrifices. This analysis involves assessing the costs of a decision against the potential benefits to ensure that the chosen strategy will provide a net positive outcome.

Example:

Marketing Budget Allocation

When a company decides how to allocate its marketing budget effectively, it must consider the strategic sacrifice involved. By carefully analysing the costs and potential returns of different marketing channels, the company can boldly reduce spending on less effective channels to invest more in high-impact strategies. For instance, shifting the budget from traditional advertising to digital marketing campaigns might result in better targeting, higher engagement, and increased sales, demonstrating a strategic sacrifice of lower-impact channels for more significant overall gain.

Example:

Talent Management

When an organisation is considering its talent management strategy, it might choose to invest in the professional development of critical employees rather than offering higher salaries across the board. This decision involves a strategic sacrifice of immediate salary increases for the more substantial benefit of a more vital, capable workforce. The company can enhance its skills and capabilities by developing high-potential employees through training and leadership programs, leading to more excellent long-term value and organisational success.

Fundamental Principles and Ethical Considerations

Key Principles:

Prioritization:

Identify and prioritise strategic goals to determine which sacrifices yield the most significant benefits.

Analytical Decision-Making:

Use cost-benefit analysis to assess the impact of potential sacrifices and ensure that the chosen strategy aligns with long-term objectives.

Resource Allocation:

Allocate resources effectively to maximise returns and support strategic priorities.

Ethical Considerations:

Fairness and Transparency:

Ensure that strategic sacrifices are made transparently and fairly, clearly communicating to stakeholders the rationale and expected outcomes.

Long-Term Impact:

Consider the long-term implications of sacrifices on employees, customers, and other stakeholders, ensuring that decisions align with ethical standards and do not cause undue harm.

The strategy "Sacrifice the Plum Tree in Place of the Peach" highlights the importance of making strategic sacrifices to achieve more significant objectives. By focusing on long-term gains and using cost-benefit analysis to guide decision-making, businesses can effectively manage resources and pursue goals that offer the most considerable benefits. Balancing these strategies with ethical considerations ensures that sacrifices are made responsibly and contribute positively to overall success.

Strategy 12: Seize the Opportunity to Lead a Sheep Away

Core Concept: Opportunism and Strategic Advantage

The 'Seize the Opportunity to Lead a Sheep Away' strategy is a powerful tool in the business arsenal. It involves capitalising on an opportunity to divert attention or resources from competitors or obstacles. This helps gain a strategic advantage by managing distractions and redirecting focus in ways that benefit one's position or goals.

Applications in Business and Competitive Positioning

1. Opportunism and Strategic Advantage

The power to seize opportunities and lead competitors or market dynamics away from one's core objectives can be a game-changer in business. It helps you gain a competitive edge and empowers you to manage challenges more effectively, putting you in the driver's seat of your business strategy.

Example:

Strategic Pricing and Promotions

Imagine the thrill of a company using aggressive pricing or promotional offers to draw attention away from a competitor's new product launch. The excitement of creating a compelling promotional campaign or temporary price reduction while at the same time overshadowing competitors' latest offerings can be invigorating. This strategic move allows the company to capitalise on the opportunity and strengthen its market position.

Example:

Product Differentiation

When entering a saturated market, the satisfaction of introducing a unique feature or service that differentiates your product can be immense. For instance, a new entrant in the smartphone market might focus on unique camera technology or eco-friendly materials, diverting consumer attention from competitors' standard offerings. By seizing this opportunity, you can capture market share and build a distinctive brand identity, a testament to your strategic prowess.

2. Identifying and Capturing Market Niches

Identifying and capturing market niches involves finding and targeting specific segments of the market that are underserved or overlooked by competitors. By focusing on these niches, businesses can establish themselves as leaders in particular areas and gain strategic advantages.

Example:

Specialised Products or Services

A business might identify a niche market with specific needs or preferences that mainstream providers must address adequately. For example, a company might specialise in high-performance gear for a niche sport or hobby, catering to enthusiasts with specific requirements. By targeting this niche, the company can build a loyal customer base and achieve a competitive advantage.

Example:

Localised Market Strategies

A global company might tailor its products or services to meet local market needs and preferences. For instance, a fast-food chain might introduce region-specific menu items that appeal to local tastes. By capturing these localised niches, the company can enhance its market relevance and attract customers who seek products that resonate with their cultural or regional preferences.

Fundamental Principles and Ethical Considerations

Key Principles:

Strategic Opportunism:

Be alert to opportunities that can provide a strategic advantage and act decisively to leverage them effectively.

Market Awareness:

Monitor market dynamics and competitor activities to identify and seize advantageous opportunities.

Focused Targeting:

Identify and target specific market niches where your business can offer unique value and gain a competitive edge.

Ethical Considerations:

Fair Competition:

Ensure that opportunistic actions do not involve unfair practices or harm competitors in ways that violate ethical standards.

Customer Trust:

Build and maintain customer trust by offering genuine value and addressing their needs effectively rather than relying solely on opportunistic tactics.

The strategy "Seize the Opportunity to Lead a Sheep Away" underscores the importance of opportunism and strategic advantage in business. Businesses can capture market niches and enhance their strategic position by identifying and leveraging opportunities to divert attention or resources from competitors. Balancing these tactics with ethical considerations ensures that strategies contribute positively to overall success and maintain fair competition in the market.

to distribute its products rather than building its distribution system. This strategy allows the startup to quickly and cost-effectively access a broader market using the existing retail chain infrastructure.

Example:

Adopting Industry Standards

A business might adopt industry-standard technologies or platforms to streamline operations and reduce development time. For example, a software company might use a widely adopted cloud computing platform to host its applications rather than develop its cloud infrastructure. This approach provides reliable and scalable solutions while focusing resources on core business activities.

2. Strategic Alliances and Synergies

Strategic alliances and synergies involve collaborating with other organisations or leveraging their assets to achieve mutual benefits. By forming partnerships or alliances, businesses can access resources, knowledge, or market positions that would be challenging to develop independently.

Example:

Joint Ventures

A company might join a joint venture with another firm to leverage each other's strengths and resources. For example, an automotive manufacturer might partner with a technology firm to develop advanced driver-assistance systems (ADAS). By combining the automotive manufacturer's industry knowledge with the technology firm's expertise, companies can achieve technological advancements and market success more effectively.

Example:

Licensing Agreements

A company might enter into licensing agreements to utilise patented technologies or intellectual property owned by others. For instance, a pharmaceutical company might license a drug formulation from another company to expedite the development and commercialisation process. This strategy allows the company to benefit from existing innovations while focusing on its core activities.

Fundamental Principles and Ethical Considerations

Key Principles:

Efficiency and Cost-Effectiveness:

Leverage existing infrastructure and resources to achieve goals efficiently and cost-effectively. Avoid duplicating efforts or investing in unnecessary developments.

Mutual Benefit:

Strategy 13: Beat the Grass to Startle the Snake

Core Concept: Testing and Provocation

The strategy "Beat the Grass to Startle the Snake" involves actions designed to provoke a response or reveal hidden aspects of a situation. This approach can be used to test reactions, uncover hidden issues, or gauge the behaviour of competitors or market forces. Initiating provocations or tests can gather valuable information and insights that inform strategic decisions.

Applications in Business and Competitive Positioning

1. Testing and Provocation

In business, testing and provocation can assess market conditions, gauge competitor responses, and gather intelligence. This involves initiating actions or scenarios intended to elicit reactions or uncover information.

Example:

Competitive Intelligence

A company might launch a limited-edition product or marketing campaign to observe competitors' reactions and gather intelligence on their strategies. For instance, a tech company could release a teaser about a potential new technology to see how competitors respond to their own product development or marketing efforts. This information can then be used to refine the company's strategy and stay ahead in the market.

Example:

Internal Testing

A company might conduct internal tests or pilot programs to gauge employee reactions and gather feedback before a full-scale rollout. For example, a company considering a significant change in its internal processes might introduce a change in a small department. By observing how employees react and adapt, the company can identify potential issues and refine the implementation plan before a wider launch.

2. Market Testing and Competitive Response

Market testing, a vital component of the 'Beat the Grass to Startle the Snake' strategy, involves introducing products, services, or marketing tactics in a controlled manner to observe consumer responses and competitive reactions. This approach gives businesses valuable insights into market dynamics and helps them make informed decisions based on actual data.

Example:

Product Beta Testing

Before a full product launch, a company might release a beta version to a select group of users. This testing phase allows the company to gather feedback on product performance, user experience, and potential issues. Observing how users interact with the product can provide valuable insights into needed improvements and how the product might be received in the broader market.

Example:

Strategic Pricing Trials

A company might experiment with pricing strategies in specific markets or segments to assess how price changes impact sales and competitor behaviour. For example, a retailer might test discount pricing in select locations to observe consumer reactions and evaluate whether competitors adjust their pricing in response. The data gathered can help the company develop more effective pricing strategies and understand market elasticity.

Fundamental Principles and Ethical Considerations

Key Principles:

Strategic Testing:

Use testing and provocation strategically to gather actionable insights and inform decision-making.

Data-Driven Decisions:

These decisions are based on the data and feedback gathered from tests and provocations to ensure informed and effective strategies.

Observational Rigor:

Ensure thorough observation and analysis of reactions to interpret the results and implications accurately.

Ethical Considerations:

Transparency and Integrity:

Conduct tests and provocations transparently and ethically, avoiding deceptive or manipulative practices that could harm stakeholders or undermine trust.

Respect for Participants:

Ensure that participants in tests or trials are treated fairly and respectfully, and their feedback is used responsibly and ethically.

The "Beat the Grass to Startle the Snake" strategy highlights the importance of testing and provocation in strategic decision-making. Businesses can uncover hidden insights, assess competitive dynamics, and refine their strategy by taking deliberate actions to provoke responses and gather information. Balancing these approaches with ethical considerations ensures that strategies are implemented effectively and responsibly.

Strategy 14: Borrow a Corpse to Raise the Spirit

Core Concept: Reviving Old Ideas for New Uses

The "Borrow a Corpse to Raise the Spirit" strategy involves revitalising an existing, often outdated or forgotten idea, concept, or product for a new purpose or context. This approach leverages the value of past innovations or trends to create something fresh and relevant, breathing new life into concepts that may need to be noticed or discarded.

Applications in Business and Competitive Positioning

1. Reviving Old Ideas for New Uses

In business, reviving old ideas can effectively capitalise on past innovations or trends, adapting them to current market conditions or consumer preferences.

Example:

Classic Product Reboots

A company might return a classic product or brand with updated features or modern design elements. For instance, a fashion brand might reintroduce a vintage clothing line with contemporary materials and styling. This approach can appeal to nostalgic customers and new audiences who appreciate the blend of old and new.

Example:

Legacy Technology

Tech companies might repurpose older technologies or concepts to address current needs. For example, the resurgence of vinyl records in the music industry illustrates how an older technology has been revitalised to meet contemporary consumer demand for nostalgic and high-quality audio experiences. Similarly, a company could adopt older software frameworks or methodologies to develop new, innovative applications.

2. Innovation through Retro and Vintage Trends

Incorporating retro and vintage trends can be a powerful way to connect with consumers and differentiate products or services. By drawing inspiration from past trends, businesses can create unique offerings that resonate with nostalgic and modern sensibilities.

Example:

Retro Marketing Campaigns

A brand might use retro-themed marketing campaigns to evoke nostalgia and create a distinctive brand identity. For instance, a beverage company might launch a limited-edition product with vintage packaging and advertising reminiscent of the 1980s.

This strategy can attract consumers with fond memories of the past while appealing to younger audiences interested in retro trends.

Example:

Vintage-Inspired Design

Designing new products with vintage-inspired aesthetics can be an effective way to capture consumer interest. For example, a furniture company might produce new pieces that mimic the style and craftsmanship of mid-century modern furniture. The company can offer products that appeal to nostalgic and design-conscious consumers by blending classic design elements with contemporary functionality.

Fundamental Principles and Ethical Considerations

Key Principles:

Relevance and Adaptation:

Ensure revived ideas or vintage elements are adapted to market needs and consumer preferences. The goal is to make them relevant and valuable in today's context.

Innovation and Freshness:

Combine old ideas with innovative elements to create something new and exciting. This approach can enhance the appeal and functionality of the revived concept.

Market Research:

Conduct thorough market research to understand how revived ideas will be received and ensure they align with current trends and consumer expectations.

Ethical Considerations:

Authenticity and Respect:

When reviving old ideas or trends, respect the concepts' original context and authenticity. Avoid appropriating or misrepresenting historical or cultural elements.

Transparency:

Communicate the origins and updates of revived products or ideas to consumers, ensuring transparency and fostering trust.

The "Borrow a Corpse to Raise the Spirit" strategy illustrates the potential of reviving and modernising old ideas to create new value and appeal. By leveraging past innovations or trends, businesses can offer unique products and experiences that resonate with consumers. Balancing this approach with thoughtful adaptation and ethical considerations ensures that the revitalised ideas are innovative and respectful of their origins.

Strategy 15: Lure the Tiger Down the Mountain

Core Concept: Enticement and Control

The strategy "Lure the Tiger Down the Mountain" involves enticing a powerful or potentially threatening force out of its advantageous position to gain control or leverage over it. By drawing the "tiger" from a high ground or stronghold to a more manageable or vulnerable position, one can more effectively deal with it through confrontation, negotiation, or strategic manoeuvring.

Applications in Business and Competitive Positioning

1. Enticement and Control

In business, enticement and control can be used to manage competitive threats, negotiate better terms, or influence market dynamics by strategically drawing competitors or partners into more favourable scenarios for oneself.

Example:

Strategic Negotiations

A company might use incentives or favourable conditions to entice a significant competitor to participate in a joint venture or partnership. The company can draw the competitor into a collaborative arrangement to exert influence and control by offering attractive terms, such as co-branding opportunities or shared resources. For instance, a technology firm might partner with a large competitor on a new product, drawing the competitor away from a separate, potentially disruptive initiative.

Example:

Market Positioning

A business might strategically lower prices or introduce a disruptive product to draw larger competitors into a price war or market segment where it has a competitive advantage. For example, a startup might offer a highly innovative product at a lower price to force larger, established companies to compete on less favourable terms, thereby gaining market share and establishing a foothold.

2. Strategic Partnership and Collaboration

Drawing partners or stakeholders into collaborative arrangements can lead to mutually beneficial outcomes and greater control over strategic directions. Businesses can forge alliances that enhance their position and influence by enticing potential partners with opportunities or benefits.

Example:

Joint Ventures and Alliances

A company might create a joint venture or strategic alliance with a more prominent industry player to leverage the partner's resources and market presence. By offering compelling benefits such as shared technology, market access, or risk mitigation, the company can entice the partner to collaborate on projects or enter new markets together. This approach allows the company to benefit from the partner's strengths while maintaining control over critical aspects of the collaboration.

Example:

Collaborative Research and Development

Companies might lure leading research institutions or other firms into collaborative R&D projects in industries where innovation is crucial. By offering access to proprietary technology, funding, or shared expertise, a company can entice these entities to work together on groundbreaking projects. This collaboration can accelerate innovation and provide the company with valuable insights and competitive advantages while sharing the risks and rewards.

Fundamental Principles and Ethical Considerations

Key Principles:

Incentive Alignment:

Ensure that the incentives or benefits offered to entice partners or competitors align with mutual interests and goals, creating a win-win situation.

Strategic Positioning:

Draw competitors or partners into scenarios where you can effectively manage and influence outcomes to your advantage.

Value Creation:

Focus on creating genuine value for all parties involved in the collaboration or negotiation, ensuring that the arrangement is beneficial and sustainable.

Ethical Considerations:

Transparency and Fairness:

Conduct enticement and control strategies transparently and fairly, ensuring that all parties know the arrangement's terms and implications.

Respect for Competitors:

Avoid deceptive practices or manipulative tactics that could harm competitors or undermine trust in the market.

The strategy "Lure the Tiger Down the Mountain" highlights the effectiveness of enticement and control in managing competitive threats and fostering strategic partnerships. By drawing powerful forces into more manageable scenarios, businesses can enhance their influence, negotiate better terms, and achieve strategic goals. Balancing these approaches with ethical considerations ensures that strategies are implemented responsibly and lead to positive outcomes for all parties involved.

Strategy 16: To Catch Something, First Let It Go

Core Concept: Flexibility and Patience

"To Catch Something, First Let It Go" involves strategically relinquishing or temporarily letting go of an asset, opportunity, or demand to achieve a more significant objective or gain. This approach emphasises the importance of flexibility and patience in achieving long-term goals, allowing for re-engagement or capturing the desired outcome when suitable.

Applications in Business and Competitive Positioning

1. Flexibility and Patience

Flexibility and patience are crucial for navigating dynamic environments and achieving long-term business success. Businesses can reposition themselves advantageously by temporarily letting go of specific priorities or demands and ultimately achieve better results.

Example:

Strategic Withdrawal

A company might strategically withdraw from a competitive market segment to focus on a more promising or profitable area. For instance, a technology firm might exit a low-margin market to concentrate resources on developing a groundbreaking product in a high-growth sector. This temporary relinquishment allows the company to build expertise and market presence in the new area, positioning itself for tremendous success in the long term.

Example:

Adapting to Market Changes

A business might adapt its strategy to changing market conditions, even temporarily letting go of specific initiatives. For example, a company might pause expansion plans during economic downturns to conserve resources and maintain financial stability. By doing so, the company can weather the downturn and then re-engage with expansion plans once conditions improve.

2. Negotiation Tactics and Strategic Concessions

In negotiations, making strategic concessions or temporarily setting aside specific demands can be effective for achieving a more favourable outcome. This approach involves offering concessions perceived as significant to the other party while maintaining the flexibility to reintroduce or capture critical points later in the negotiation.

Example:

Negotiating Deals

During contract negotiations, a company might agree to certain concessions or compromises to move the negotiation forward. For instance, a business might decide to lower its initial price to secure a deal, understanding that it can negotiate for better terms or additional benefits in subsequent phases of the agreement. This tactic demonstrates flexibility and can help reach an agreement while preserving the opportunity to capture more value later.

Example:

Strategic Alliances

When forming strategic alliances, a company might reject demands or conditions to attract a partner or secure an agreement. By offering favourable terms or concessions upfront, the company can build goodwill and establish a strong foundation for collaboration. This initial flexibility can lead to a more fruitful partnership, with the opportunity to renegotiate terms or capture additional value as the alliance develops.

Fundamental Principles and Ethical Considerations

Key Principles:

Strategic Timing:

Use flexibility and patience to effectively time actions and concessions, ensuring they align with long-term goals and objectives.

Value Assessment:

Evaluate the benefits of resisting demands or priorities and ensure that the anticipated gains justify the trade-offs.

Adaptability:

Maintain the ability to adapt and re-engage with key objectives or opportunities when conditions are more favourable.

Ethical Considerations:

Honesty and Transparency:

Conducted negotiations and strategic concessions honestly and transparently, ensuring all parties knew the terms and implications.

Fairness:

Ensure that concessions or withdrawals are made fairly and do not disadvantage or exploit other parties involved in the negotiation or business relationship.

The strategy "To Catch Something, First Let It Go" highlights the importance of flexibility and patience in achieving strategic goals. By temporarily relinquishing demands or priorities, businesses can position themselves for tremendous success and re-engage with opportunities when right. Balancing these approaches with ethical considerations ensures that strategies are implemented effectively and responsibly, leading to favourable outcomes and sustained success.

Strategy 17: Toss out a Brick to Attract Jade

Core Concept: Offering Something Small to Gain Something Big

The "Toss Out a Brick to Attract Jade" strategy involves offering something relatively minor or low-cost to attract a more valuable opportunity or gain. This approach uses a modest offer or gesture to entice and engage others, ultimately achieving a more enormous and significant benefit.

Applications in Business and Competitive Positioning

1. Offering Something Small to Gain Something Big

In business, this strategy is often used to attract customers, partners, or opportunities by providing an initial, modest incentive that can lead to more substantial outcomes.

Example:

Free Trials and Samples

A company might offer free trials or samples of its products to attract potential customers. For example, a software company might provide a free trial period for users to experience its features and benefits. This low-cost offer can lead to higher conversion rates and customer acquisition if the product meets the users' needs and demonstrates its value.

Example:

Introductory Discounts

Retailers often use introductory discounts or promotions to attract new customers. For instance, a new restaurant might offer a discount on the first meal to draw in diners and encourage them to try the menu. Once customers are engaged and experience the service or food quality, they are more likely to return and become regular patrons.

2. Marketing and Customer Acquisition Strategies

This strategy can be effectively applied in various marketing and customer acquisition tactics to build interest and generate leads.

Example:

Lead Magnets

In digital marketing, businesses often use lead magnets—such as free e-books, webinars, or guides—to attract potential customers. For example, a marketing consultancy might offer a free downloadable guide on effective marketing strategies. The guide serves as a "brick" that captures the interest of potential clients and allows the consultancy to build a relationship, ultimately leading to more significant business engagements.

Example:

Content Marketing

Companies might create and share valuable content, such as blog posts, videos, or infographics, to attract and engage their target audience. For instance, a company specialising in home improvement might publish detailed DIY guides and tips on their website. This content acts as a "brick" to draw in readers and potential customers who may seek the company's services for more comprehensive projects.

Example:

Referral Programs

Businesses can implement referral programs that reward existing customers for bringing in new clients. For example, a subscription service might offer a discount or free month of service to customers who refer friends or family. This small incentive encourages current users to promote the service, potentially leading to a more extensive base of new subscribers.

Fundamental Principles and Ethical Considerations

Key Principles:

Value Proposition:

Ensure the small offer or incentive provides genuine value and effectively attracts the target audience.

Alignment with Goals:

Design the offer to align with broader business objectives, ensuring it leads to meaningful and desirable outcomes.

Effective Engagement:

Use the initial offer to build relationships and engage potential customers or partners in a way that fosters long-term connections.

Ethical Considerations:

Transparency:

Be transparent about the offer's terms and conditions, ensuring potential customers or partners understand what they are receiving and what is expected in return.

Fairness:

Ensure the offer is fair and does not mislead or exploit participants. The goal is to create a mutually beneficial situation rather than taking advantage of others.

The strategy "Toss Out a Brick to Attract Jade" demonstrates the effectiveness of offering something modest or low-cost to attract more significant opportunities or benefits. By using small incentives to engage and build interest, businesses can achieve essential outcomes in customer acquisition and marketing. Balancing these tactics with transparency and fairness ensures that adequate and ethical strategies lead to positive and sustainable results.

Strategy 18: To Catch the Bandits, First Capture Their Leader

Core Concept: Leadership and Influence

The strategy "To Catch the Bandits, First Capture Their Leader" focuses on addressing the root cause of a problem or challenge by targeting its most influential or central element. In this context, capturing a group's leader is crucial for dismantling the entire group's influence and operations. This principle can be applied to business and organisational settings by focusing on key leaders and influencers to drive broader change or achieve strategic objectives.

Applications in Business and Competitive Positioning

1. Leadership and Influence

Understanding and leveraging the power of leadership and influence can be instrumental in achieving strategic goals in a business setting. By addressing the key figures who have a significant impact, companies can effectively manage challenges, drive transformation, and enhance their competitive position.

Example:

Competitive Disruption

A company might target or acquire influential leaders within a competitor's organisation to gain a competitive edge in a market. For instance, a tech company might recruit top executives from a rival firm to leverage their industry knowledge and connections. The company can gain insights into the competitor's strategies, influence the market, and enhance its strategic positioning.

Example:

Transformational Leadership

Focusing on key leaders who can champion the transformation is essential to drive organisational change. For example, a company undergoing a digital transformation might prioritise engaging and empowering senior leaders who are critical in driving the change across departments. Their support and influence can help align the organisation with new technologies and practices, ensuring a smoother transition and a more significant overall impact.

2. Organisational Management and Key Talent Acquisition

Targeting key talent and influential individuals in organisational management is critical for building strong teams and achieving organisational objectives. Companies can enhance their performance and competitive advantage by recruiting or developing leaders who can drive success.

Example:

Key Talent Recruitment

A company seeking to expand into a new market might focus on recruiting key industry leaders with established reputations and networks. For instance, a financial services firm might hire a prominent figure from a competing firm with extensive experience and connections in a target region. This strategic talent acquisition can give the company valuable insights, relationships, and credibility in the new market.

Example:

Succession Planning

Effective succession planning involves identifying and developing future leaders within an organisation. By nurturing key talent and potential leaders, companies can ensure a smooth transition and continuity in leadership roles. For example, a company might implement leadership development programs to groom high-potential employees for future executive positions. This approach helps build a strong leadership pipeline and prepares the organisation for long-term success.

Fundamental Principles and Ethical Considerations

Key Principles:

Influence and Impact:

Recognise key leaders' and talent's influence and impact on organisational success and strategic objectives.

Strategic Focus:

Target influential figures strategically to address core challenges or drive significant change.

Leadership Development:

Invest in developing and empowering key leaders to enhance organisational performance and achieve goals.

Ethical Considerations:

Respect and Fairness:

Ensure that efforts to recruit or target key leaders are conducted with respect and fairness, avoiding practices that could be seen as exploitative or unethical.

Transparency:

Maintaining transparency in leadership transitions and talent acquisition ensures all parties understand the terms and implications.

The strategy "To Catch the Bandits, First Capture Their Leader" highlights the importance of addressing key sources of influence and leadership to achieve broader objectives. Businesses can effectively manage challenges, drive transformation, and build strong teams by targeting influential individuals and leveraging their impact. Balancing these approaches with respect, fairness, and transparency ensures that strategies are implemented ethically and lead to positive outcomes.

Strategy 19: Steal the Firewood from Under the Pot

Core Concept: Undermining Competitors

The strategy "Steal the Firewood from Under the Pot" involves undermining the resources or support that sustain a competitor, diminishing their ability to perform or compete effectively. By targeting the foundational elements that support a competitor's operations or success, one can gain a competitive edge and disrupt their position in the market.

Applications in Business and Competitive Positioning

1. Undermining Competitors

In business, strategically undermining competitors involves identifying and disrupting their essential resources, support systems, or advantages. This approach weakens the competitor's position, making gaining market share or achieving strategic objectives easier.

Example:

Disrupting Supply Chains

A company might use tactics to disrupt a competitor's supply chain. For instance, if a business identifies that a competitor relies on a specific supplier for critical components, it might work to secure exclusive agreements with that supplier or develop alternative supply sources. Doing so could impact the competitor's production, allowing the business to capitalise on supply chain weaknesses.

Example:

Targeted Marketing Campaigns

A company could launch targeted marketing campaigns that highlight the shortcomings or vulnerabilities of a competitor's product or service. For instance, a smartphone manufacturer might run advertisements emphasizing superior features or reliability compared to a rival brand. This strategy can erode the competitor's market position and attract customers to the company's offering.

2. Strategic Disruption and Competitive Edge

Using strategic disruption to gain a competitive edge involves creating situations that force competitors to divert resources or attention away from their core operations. This approach can enhance one's position in the market by exploiting the competitor's vulnerabilities.

Example:

Market Innovation

A company might introduce a disruptive innovation that shifts market dynamics and forces competitors to adapt quickly. For instance, competitors may struggle to keep up or invest heavily to catch up if a company launches a groundbreaking technology or service that changes consumer expectations. This disruption can create a competitive advantage for the innovating company and attract customers seeking the latest advancements.

Example:

Strategic Alliances

Strategic alliances or partnerships with key industry players can undermine competitors by enhancing one's market position and influence. For example, businesses might partner with influential retailers or technology providers to gain preferential market access or resources. This alliance can weaken competitors who do not have similar partnerships, providing a competitive edge.

Fundamental Principles and Ethical Considerations

Key Principles:

Strategic Focus:

Identify and target the essential resources or support systems critical to competitors' success. Disrupt these elements to gain a competitive advantage.

Innovation and Adaptation:

Use innovation and strategic moves to disrupt competitors' positions and shift market dynamics in your favour.

Resource Efficiency:

Ensure efforts to undermine competitors are efficient and effectively directed toward achieving strategic goals.

Ethical Considerations:

Fair Competition:

Conduct competitive strategies fairly and ethically, avoiding practices that could be considered underhanded or deceptive.

Respect for Competitors:

Respect competitors' rights and avoid actions that could harm their operations or reputation in an unethical way.

The strategy "Steal the Firewood from Under the Pot" emphasises the importance of undermining competitors' critical resources and support systems to gain a competitive edge. Businesses can enhance their market position by strategically disrupting a competitor's foundation and achieving tremendous success. Balancing these tactics with ethical considerations ensures that competitive strategies are implemented responsibly and lead to sustainable outcomes.

Strategy 20: Trouble the Water to Catch the Fish

Core Concept: Creating Chaos to Control

The strategy "Trouble the Water to Catch the Fish" involves creating confusion or disturbance to gain control or advantage. By introducing uncertainty or disrupting the status quo, one can manipulate the environment to capture opportunities or achieve desired outcomes. This approach leverages the resulting chaos to gain the upper hand.

Applications in Business and Competitive Positioning

1. Creating Chaos to Control

In a business context, creating chaos can be a strategic manoeuvre to unsettle competitors, disrupt market dynamics, or shift focus on one's favour. This tactic can be used to create openings for new opportunities or to influence the behaviour of competitors and stakeholders.

Example:

Competitive Disruption

A company might introduce disruptive innovations or unexpected changes to unsettle competitors. For instance, a technology firm could launch a new product or service with groundbreaking features that challenge existing market leaders. This move can create confusion and force competitors to react, potentially giving the innovating company a chance to capture market share or reshape industry standards.

Example:

Strategic PR Campaigns

A business might use strategic public relations campaigns to create buzz and shift public attention. For example, a company could launch a controversial marketing campaign or release a provocative statement that generates widespread discussion and media coverage. This approach can divert attention from competitors and position the company as a thought leader or innovator.

2. Crisis and Opportunity Management

Troubling the water can also be applied in managing crises and seizing opportunities that arise from turbulent situations. Businesses can turn challenges into strategic advantages by effectively navigating and capitalising on chaos.

Example:

Crisis Response

During a market crisis or industry upheaval, a company might adopt a bold response strategy to capitalise on the situation. For example, a retailer facing supply chain disruptions might use the opportunity to pivot towards a new business model, such as enhancing its online presence or offering new product lines. The company can address the crisis effectively and emerge more decisive in the market.

Example:

Acquisition Opportunities

Companies can identify and acquire undervalued assets or distressed competitors in market instability. For instance, a company might acquire struggling firms during an economic downturn at favourable terms. This strategy allows the acquiring company to strengthen its market position and expand its capabilities while competitors are preoccupied with managing crises.

Fundamental Principles and Ethical Considerations

Key Principles:

Strategic Intent:

Ensure that the creation of chaos or disturbance aligns with broader strategic goals and objectives and is used to gain a meaningful advantage.

Opportunity Identification:

Identify and capitalise on opportunities that arise from disruptive situations, using the chaos to shift focus or create openings.

Crisis Management:

Manage crises effectively by turning challenges into opportunities and maintaining control over the situation to achieve desired outcomes.

Ethical Considerations:

Ethical Disruption:

Ensure that chaos is created ethically and does not involve deceptive or harmful practices that could negatively impact stakeholders or competitors.

Responsibility:

Consider the broader implications of disrupting the status quo and ensure that actions are responsible and do not cause undue harm or instability.

The strategy "Trouble the Water to Catch the Fish" illustrates how creating disturbance or confusion can be used to gain control and capture opportunities. By strategically introducing chaos, businesses can influence market dynamics, disrupt competitors, and turn challenging situations into advantages. Balancing these tactics with ethical considerations ensures that strategies are implemented responsibly and lead to positive, sustainable outcomes.

Strategy 21: Shed Your Skin Like the Golden Cicada

Core Concept: Transformation and Reinvention

The strategy "Shed Your Skin Like the Golden Cicada" involves undergoing a significant transformation or reinvention to escape undesirable situations or to reposition oneself for new opportunities. Just as the golden cicada sheds its old skin to renew itself, businesses and individuals can adopt this strategy to refresh their image, adapt to changes, and seize new prospects.

Applications in Business and Competitive Positioning

1. Transformation and Reinvention

Transformation and reinvention are crucial for staying relevant and competitive in evolving markets. Businesses can navigate challenges and unlock new opportunities by effectively managing change and embracing new identities or approaches.

Example:

Corporate Turnarounds

A company experiencing declining performance might transform significantly to revitalise its brand and operations. For instance, a traditional retail company facing declining sales might reinvent itself by embracing e-commerce, updating its product lines, and modernising its brand image. This transformation helps the company adapt to changing consumer preferences and regain market relevance.

Example:

Adapting to Market Changes

A company might pivot its business model or product offerings in response to market trends or technological advancements. For example, a print media company might transition to a digital-first strategy by investing in online content, digital marketing, and data analytics. This strategic reinvention allows the company to remain competitive in the digital age and attract a new audience.

2. Personal and Corporate Rebranding

Personal and corporate rebranding involves updating and repositioning one's image or identity to align with current goals and market conditions. This strategy can help individuals and organisations present themselves more effectively and capture new opportunities.

Example:

Personal Career Rebranding

Individuals seeking to advance their careers might undergo a personal rebranding to enhance their professional image and open new doors. This could involve updating their resume, improving their online presence, and acquiring new skills or certifications. For example, a professional transitioning from a traditional industry to a tech-focused role might rebrand themselves as a tech-savvy expert by highlighting relevant experience and education.

Example:

Corporate Rebranding

A company might rebrand to refresh its image, address negative perceptions, or appeal to a new customer segment. For instance, a legacy brand might undertake rebranding, including a new logo, updated marketing materials, and a revised mission statement. This rebranding effort helps the company signal a new direction and attract a modern audience while shedding outdated or negative associations.

Fundamental Principles and Ethical Considerations

Key Principles:

Strategic Alignment:

Ensure that transformation or rebranding efforts align with broader strategic goals and objectives. The changes should be purposeful and support long-term vision.

Authenticity:

Maintain authenticity throughout the transformation or rebranding process. Ensure that new identities or approaches reflect valid values and capabilities.

Stakeholder Communication:

Communicate changes effectively to stakeholders, including customers, employees, and partners, to ensure a smooth transition and build support for the new direction.

Ethical Considerations:

Transparency:

Be transparent about the reasons for transformation or rebranding and avoid misleading stakeholders about the nature or extent of the changes.

Responsibility:

Ensure that the rebranding or transformation efforts do not involve deceptive practices or cause undue harm to others. The goal is to create positive and constructive change.

The strategy "Shed Your Skin Like the Golden Cicada" highlights the importance of transformation and reinvention in achieving new opportunities and adapting to change. By embracing strategic change and rebranding efforts, businesses and individuals can effectively navigate evolving environments and position themselves for success. Balancing these approaches with authenticity, strategic alignment, and transparency ensures that transformation leads to positive, sustainable outcomes.

Strategy 22: Shut the Door to Catch the Thief

Core Concept: Control and Security

The "Shut the Door to Catch the Thief" strategy involves implementing measures to effectively control access and secure a situation to address a problem or threat. By closing avenues for unauthorised access or potential threats, one can more effectively manage and resolve issues, ensuring that problems are contained and addressed.

Applications in Business and Competitive Positioning

1. Control and Security

In business, ensuring control and security involves creating barriers or implementing safeguards to protect assets, information, and operations from potential threats or unauthorised access. This approach helps manage risks and maintain operational integrity.

Example:

Cybersecurity Measures

A company might enhance its cybersecurity protocols to protect against data breaches and unauthorised access. This could involve implementing strong password policies, encryption, multi-factor authentication, and regular security audits. By "shutting the door" on potential cyber threats, the company secures its sensitive data and minimises the risk of breaches.

Example:

Physical Security Enhancements

Businesses with valuable assets or sensitive information might invest in physical security measures such as access control systems, surveillance cameras, and security personnel. For instance, a high-value manufacturing facility might implement secure entry points and monitor access to prevent theft or sabotage. This proactive approach helps protect the company's assets and ensures safe operations.

2. Risk Management and Crisis Containment

Effective risk management and crisis containment involve identifying potential risks and implementing strategies to control and mitigate them. By addressing threats or vulnerabilities proactively, businesses can minimise the impact of crises and ensure a swift resolution.

Example:

Contingency Planning

A company might develop comprehensive contingency plans to address potential crises or emergencies. For example, an organisation might create a detailed response plan for natural disasters, supply chain disruptions, or financial crises. The company can respond effectively and minimise disruptions by planning for various scenarios and "shutting the door" on potential threats.

Example:

Legal and Compliance Controls

Implementing robust legal and compliance controls helps businesses manage risks related to regulatory compliance and legal issues. For instance, a company might establish strict compliance protocols and conduct regular audits to ensure adherence to industry regulations. This approach helps "shut the door" on legal risks and avoids potential penalties or legal disputes.

Fundamental Principles and Ethical Considerations

Key Principles:

- **Proactive Measures**:
- Implement proactive measures to control access, secure assets, and manage risks effectively. Anticipate potential threats and address them before they escalate.
- **Comprehensive Security**:
- Ensure that security measures are extensive and address risk management's physical and digital aspects.
- **Crisis Preparedness**:
- Develop and maintain contingency plans to respond effectively to crises and minimise impact.

Ethical Considerations:

- **Transparency and Fairness**:
- Ensure that security measures and risk management strategies are transparent and fair, avoiding practices that could infringe on privacy or cause undue harm.
- **Responsibility**:
- Implement adequate controls and safeguards to protect stakeholders and ensure ethical management of risks.

The strategy "Shut the Door to Catch the Thief" underscores the importance of control and security in managing risks and addressing threats. By implementing measures to prevent unauthorised access and secure critical assets, businesses can effectively manage potential problems and ensure operational integrity. Balancing these strategies with transparency, fairness, and comprehensive planning ensures that risk management efforts lead to positive and sustainable outcomes.

Strategy 23: Befriend a Distant Enemy to Attack One Nearby

Core Concept: Strategic Alliances and Rivalry

The strategy "Befriend a Distant Enemy to Attack One Nearby" involves forming alliances or building relationships with distant or less immediate opponents to create strategic advantages for tackling more immediate or pressing rivals. By leveraging relationships with distant entities, one can focus resources and efforts on more immediate challenges or competitors, gaining an upper hand in the process.

Applications in Business and Competitive Positioning

1. Strategic Alliances and Rivalry

Forging alliances with distant or less direct competitors can provide strategic advantages and create opportunities to address more immediate threats. These alliances can help manage competitive dynamics and optimise resource allocation.

Example:

Strategic Partnerships

A company facing intense competition in its core market might form strategic partnerships with businesses in adjacent or unrelated industries. For instance, a tech company struggling with market competition might collaborate with a research institution or an international technology firm. This alliance can provide access to new technologies, markets, or resources, allowing the company to better compete against immediate rivals.

Example:

Trade Associations

Businesses might join trade associations or industry groups to build relationships with distant competitors or stakeholders. By participating in industry-wide initiatives or forums, a company can gain insights, influence industry standards, and form alliances that indirectly support its position against more immediate competitors.

2. Diplomacy and Competitive Strategy

Effective diplomacy and competitive strategy involve managing relationships and leveraging alliances to gain strategic advantages. Businesses can use diplomatic approaches to form beneficial connections to enhance their position and effectively address competitive challenges.

Example:

Negotiating Market Entry

A company seeking to enter a new international market might establish partnerships or alliances with local businesses or government entities. For example, an American company aiming to expand into Asia might collaborate with a local distributor or joint venture partner. This diplomatic approach can help navigate regulatory challenges and build market presence while focusing resources on competing with regional rivals.

Example:

Cross-Industry Collaboration

A company might engage in cross-industry collaborations to address competitive pressures. For instance, a pharmaceutical company might partner with a biotechnology firm to co-develop new treatments. By building relationships with distant players in the industry, the company can enhance its capabilities and focus on competing more effectively in its primary market.

Fundamental Principles and Ethical Considerations

Key Principles:

Strategic Alignment:

Ensure that alliances and relationships with distant entities align with overall strategic goals and provide meaningful benefits for addressing immediate challenges.

Resource Optimization:

Use strategic alliances to optimise resource allocation and focus on more critical competitive threats.

Diplomatic Approach:

Employ diplomatic and collaborative approaches to build beneficial relationships and gain strategic advantages.

Ethical Considerations:

Transparency:

Maintain transparency in forming alliances and relationships, ensuring that all parties understand the terms and intentions of the collaboration.

Fair Play:

Ensure that alliances and competitive strategies are conducted ethically, avoiding practices seen as manipulative or deceptive.

Responsibility:

Consider the broader impact of strategic alliances and ensure they contribute to positive outcomes for stakeholders and the industry.

The strategy "Befriend a Distant Enemy to Attack One Nearby" emphasises the importance of leveraging strategic alliances and diplomatic approaches to gain an advantage over more immediate rivals. By building relationships with distant entities, businesses can enhance their position and focus on addressing pressing competitive challenges. Balancing these strategies with transparency, strategic alignment, and ethical considerations ensures that alliances contribute to sustainable and positive outcomes.

Strategy 24: Borrow the Road to Conquer Guo

Core Concept: Leveraging Existing Infrastructure

The strategy "Borrow the Road to Conquer Guo" involves utilising existing resources, systems, or infrastructures to achieve one's objectives rather than relying solely on building new capabilities from scratch. By leveraging the assets and pathways already established by others, one can efficiently pursue goals and expand influence.

Applications in Business and Competitive Positioning

1. Leveraging Existing Infrastructure

In business, leveraging existing infrastructure means leveraging established systems, networks, or resources to enhance one's capabilities or achieve strategic objectives. This approach can lead to significant efficiencies and cost savings.

Example:

Utilising Distribution Channels

A company might partner with established distribution networks to reach new markets or customer segments. For instance, a startup company could collaborate with a well-established retail chain

Ensure that alliances and partnerships provide mutual benefits and align with strategic objectives. Both parties should gain value from the collaboration.

Strategic Alignment:

Align the use of existing resources or partnerships with overall strategic goals and ensure that they support long-term objectives.

Ethical Considerations:

Fairness and Transparency:

Conduct partnerships and collaborations transparently and fairly, ensuring that all parties understand the terms and benefits of the arrangement.

Respect for Intellectual Property:

Respect intellectual property rights and ensure that licensing or borrowing agreements are conducted ethically and legally.

Responsible Use:

Use existing resources and partnerships responsibly, ensuring the approach does not undermine other stakeholders' interests or create potentially problematic dependencies.

The "Borrow the Road to Conquer Guo" strategy highlights the value of leveraging existing infrastructure and forming strategic alliances to achieve more effective objectives. By utilising established systems and collaborating with others, businesses can enhance their capabilities, reduce costs, and accelerate progress. Balancing these strategies with fairness, strategic alignment, and ethical considerations ensures that the approach leads to positive and sustainable outcomes.

Strategy 25: Replace the Beams with Rotten Timbers

Core Concept: Sabotage and Deception

The "Replace the Beams with Rotten Timbers" strategy involves undermining an opponent's foundational support systems or resources by subtly introducing flaws or weaknesses. This tactic aims to create vulnerabilities that can be exploited, causing disruption or failure from within. The strategy leverages deception and indirect actions to weaken competitors or market entrants.

Applications in Business and Competitive Positioning

1. Sabotage and Deception

In business, sabotage and deception involve subtly undermining a competitor's operations or reputation to gain a strategic advantage. This approach can disrupt a competitor's performance or create opportunities for one's own business.

Example:

Market Disruption

A company might engage in practices designed to disrupt a competitor's operations. For instance, a business might spread misinformation about a competitor's product quality or service reliability.

This could lead to customer dissatisfaction and loss of market share for the competitor, creating an opportunity for the business to capture those customers.

Example:

Undermining Supply Chains

A company might exploit weaknesses in a competitor's supply chain by strategically influencing suppliers or logistics providers. For example, suppose a competitor is reliant on a specific supplier. In that case, one might work to create delays or issues with that supplier, indirectly impacting the competitor's ability to deliver products on time.

2. Disrupting Competitors and Market Entrants

Disrupting competitors or new market entrants involves creating obstacles or vulnerabilities that hinder their ability to compete effectively. By strategically introducing weaknesses, one can reduce the competitive pressure and create openings for their business.

Example:

Competitive Intelligence

A company might use competitive intelligence to identify and exploit weaknesses in a competitor's business model or strategy. For instance, by analysing a competitor's pricing strategy or operational inefficiencies, a business could design targeted actions that exploit those weaknesses, such as undercutting prices in critical areas or offering superior alternatives.

Example:

Regulatory and Compliance Challenges

A business might seek to introduce regulatory or compliance challenges for new market entrants. For example, by highlighting potential regulatory issues or non-compliance concerns, a company can create obstacles for competitors trying to enter the market. This approach can impede their progress, providing an advantage to the established business.

Fundamental Principles and Ethical Considerations

Key Principles:

Strategic Impact:

Ensure that any actions to undermine competitors or market entrants are strategically sound and align with broader business objectives.

Discreet Execution:

Implement sabotage or disruption tactics to minimise risk to one's own business and maintain a focus on achieving long-term goals.

Competitive Analysis:

Use competitive intelligence and analysis to identify and exploit vulnerabilities, ensuring that tactics are well-informed and targeted.

Ethical Considerations:

Fair Competition:

Ensure that competitive actions do not involve unethical or illegal practices. Avoid tactics that could be deemed deceptive or harmful beyond acceptable business conduct.

Transparency and Integrity:

Maintain openness and integrity in business operations, ensuring that actions taken to disrupt competitors are consistent with ethical standards.

Long-Term Impact:

Consider the long-term impact of sabotage or disruption tactics on industry reputation and stakeholder relationships.

The strategy "Replace the Beams with Rotten Timbers" highlights the use of subtle sabotage and deception to undermine competitors and disrupt market entrants. Businesses can gain a competitive advantage by strategically introducing weaknesses, creating obstacles, and influencing market dynamics. Balancing these tactics with ethical considerations and strategic objectives ensures that competitive actions lead to sustainable and positive outcomes.

Strategy 26: Point at the Mulberry but Curse the Locust Tree

Core Concept: Indirect Criticism and Influence

The "Point at the Mulberry but Curse the Locust Tree" strategy involves directing criticism or negative comments toward a less relevant target while addressing or influencing the real issue. This approach uses indirect methods to express dissatisfaction or influence opinions without confronting the primary target directly. It allows for subtle communication and strategic influence while avoiding confrontation.

Applications in Business and Competitive Positioning

1. Indirect Criticism and Influence

In business, indirect criticism involves addressing issues or concerns that avoid confrontation but influence the intended target. This approach can help navigate sensitive topics, manage stakeholder relationships, or subtly influence opinions.

Example:

Public Relations and Media

A company might use public statements or media campaigns to indirectly address criticism or competitor weaknesses without naming specific rivals. For instance, a tech company might release a public statement about industry-wide issues related to data privacy without directly naming a competitor known for data breaches. This indirect approach allows the company to position itself as a leader in privacy without engaging in direct attacks.

Example:

Internal Feedback

In a corporate setting, an executive might provide feedback to a team indirectly by discussing general industry trends or challenges rather than targeting specific team members or departments. For instance, if a team's performance is lacking, the executive might discuss industry-wide best practices or standards in a meeting, subtly guiding the team toward improved performance without directly criticising individuals.

2. Communication Strategies and Diplomatic Language

Effective communication strategies and diplomatic language involve subtlety and indirect approaches to address sensitive issues or influence opinions. This approach can help manage conflicts, build consensus, and achieve goals without confrontation.

Example:

Diplomatic Negotiations

Representatives might use diplomatic language to address contentious issues in diplomatic negotiations or business discussions. For example, during negotiations, a party might use terms like "areas for improvement" or "growth opportunities" to address concerns about the other party's proposals rather than making direct criticisms. This indirect approach helps maintain a positive tone while addressing underlying issues.

Example:

Brand Messaging

A company might use brand messaging to position itself against competitors without explicit comparison. For instance, a brand promoting its products as "more sustainable" might indirectly critique competitors that are less focused on sustainability. The brand influences perceptions without directly attacking others by emphasising its strengths in a particular area.

Fundamental Principles and Ethical Considerations

Key Principles:

Subtle Influence:

Use indirect methods to address concerns or influence opinions while avoiding confrontation or negative relationship impacts.

Strategic Communication:

Employ strategic communication and diplomatic language to manage sensitive topics effectively and achieve desired outcomes.

Focus on Goals:

Ensure that indirect criticism or influence aligns with broader strategic goals and contributes to achieving objectives.

Ethical Considerations:

Respect and Integrity:

Maintain respect and integrity in indirect communication, avoiding misleading or deceptive practices. Ensure that criticism is constructive and relevant.

Transparency:

When using indirect methods, be transparent about intentions and objectives, ensuring that actions are ethical and contribute to positive outcomes.

Responsibility:

Consider the impact of indirect criticism on stakeholders and ensure that communication strategies are responsible and do not create undue harm.

The "Point at the Mulberry but Curse the Locust Tree" strategy emphasises indirect criticism and diplomatic language to address issues or influence opinions subtly. Businesses and individuals can navigate sensitive topics, manage relationships, and achieve objectives without confrontation by strategically directing criticism and nuanced communication. Balancing these approaches with respect, transparency, and ethical considerations ensures that communication strategies are practical and constructive.

Strategy 27: Feign Madness, But Keep Your Balance

Core Concept: Strategic Disguise and Misleading

The strategy "Feign Madness but Keep Your Balance" involves adopting seemingly irrational or unpredictable behaviour to mislead others while maintaining control and balance. This approach uses strategic disguises to create confusion or misinterpretation, allowing one to achieve objectives by manipulating perceptions and expectations.

Applications in Business and Competitive Positioning

1. Strategic Disguise and Misleading

In business, employing a strategic disguise or misleading behaviour involves creating a façade or using unconventional tactics to achieve strategic objectives. This can be useful for gaining a competitive edge, misdirecting rivals, or managing market perceptions.

Example:

Market Positioning

A company might adopt a seemingly unconventional or unpredictable marketing approach to create buzz and intrigue. For instance, a tech startup might launch a series of enigmatic advertisements or product teasers that appear irrational but generate significant media attention and consumer curiosity. While the initial behaviour may seem erratic, it is strategically designed to draw attention and differentiate the company from competitors.

Example:

Negotiation Tactics

During negotiations, a party might adopt a seemingly irrational stance or make unconventional demands to create confusion and gain leverage. For instance, a company might appear overly demanding or uncooperative in early negotiations to test the boundaries and gauge the other party's flexibility. This approach can lead to better terms and concessions once the position is revealed.

2. Managing Perceptions and Expectations

Managing perceptions and expectations involves using strategic behaviour to influence how others view a situation or individual. By carefully controlling how one is perceived, businesses and individuals can shape outcomes and navigate complex scenarios more effectively.

Example:

Competitive Strategy

A company might deliberately underperform or downplay its capabilities to set low expectations among competitors or stakeholders. For example, a company entering a new market might initially present as a minor player or adopt a low-profile approach. As competitors and customers underestimate its potential, the company can execute a more aggressive strategy or unveil its true strengths, gaining an advantage.

Example:

Personal Branding

An individual might adopt a seemingly unconventional or quirky personal brand to stand out and capture attention. For example, a professional might cultivate a unique or eccentric public persona to differentiate themselves from others. While their behaviour might seem unusual, it is strategically designed to create a memorable and distinct personal brand that attracts opportunities.

Fundamental Principles and Ethical Considerations

Key Principles:

Controlled Behaviour:

Ensure that any use of strategic disguise or misleading behaviour is carefully controlled and purposeful. Avoid actions that could lead to unintended negative consequences.

Perception Management:

Use strategic behaviour to manage perceptions and expectations effectively, aligning with overall objectives and long-term goals.

Flexibility:

Maintain balance and control despite adopting seemingly irrational behaviour, ensuring that the strategic approach does not compromise core values or objectives.

Ethical Considerations:

Transparency and Honesty:

Avoid practices that involve deception or dishonesty. Ensure that strategic disguise does not mislead or harm others beyond acceptable boundaries.

Respect for Others:

Consider the impact of strategic behaviour on other stakeholders and maintain respect and professionalism in interactions.

Long-Term Impact:

Evaluate the long-term impact of using strategic disguises or misleading behaviour, ensuring that it contributes to sustainable and positive outcomes.

The strategy "Feign Madness but Keep Your Balance" highlights using strategic disguises and misleading behaviour to influence perceptions and achieve objectives. By adopting seemingly irrational tactics while maintaining control, businesses and individuals can navigate complex scenarios, gain competitive advantages, and manage expectations effectively. Balancing these approaches with ethical considerations and long-term goals ensures that strategies are effective, respectful, and sustainable.

Strategy 28: Lure Your Enemy onto the Roof, Then Take Away the Ladder

Core Concept: Entrapment and Control

The strategy "Lure Your Enemy onto the Roof, Then Take Away the Ladder" involves enticing an opponent into a position where they are vulnerable or have limited options and removing their means of escape or counteraction. This approach uses entrapment and control to force the opponent into a disadvantageous position, making it difficult for them to recover or retaliate.

Applications in Business and Competitive Positioning

1. Entrapment and Control

In business, entrapment and control create scenarios where competitors or market players are placed in challenging positions with limited options. This can be achieved through strategic positioning, resource control, or market manipulation.

Example:

Market Saturation

A company might strategically flood a market with aggressive pricing, promotions, or new product offerings to force competitors into a difficult position. For instance, a tech company might introduce low-cost, high-value products to corner a market segment. Competitors, unable to compete on price or innovation, may find themselves in a precarious position with few options for response.

Example:

Resource Dependency

A business might strategically position itself as a critical supplier or partner for competitors. For example, a company could become a key provider of essential components or services that competitors rely on. By controlling these critical resources, the company can exert influence and limit the competitors' ability to operate effectively.

2. Negotiation and Competitive Positioning

In negotiation and competitive scenarios, this strategy involves manoeuvring opponents or partners into positions where they are at a disadvantage and then leveraging that position to achieve favourable terms or outcomes.

Example:

Negotiation Leverage

In a negotiation, one party might initially agree to seemingly generous terms to gain trust or cooperation from the other party. Once the other party is fully committed and invested in the arrangement, the first party can shift the terms or introduce new conditions favouring their position. For example, a company might agree to a partnership with a favourable initial agreement, only to introduce less favourable terms later once the partner is heavily invested and dependent on the partnership.

Example:

Competitive Manoeuvring

A business might use competitive manoeuvres to isolate a rival. For instance, a company could strategically acquire critical suppliers or partners that a competitor relies on. By doing so, the company limits competitors' options and operational flexibility, making it challenging for them to compete effectively.

Fundamental Principles and Ethical Considerations

Key Principles:

Strategic Positioning:

Ensure entrapment or control tactics are strategically sound and aligned with overall business objectives. Focus on creating genuine competitive advantages rather than short-term gains.

Leverage and Influence:

Use entrapment and control to gain leverage and influence in negotiations or competitive scenarios.

Ensure that actions are deliberate and well-planned to maximise effectiveness.

Resource Management:

Manage critical resources or positions to create strategic advantages while maintaining long-term sustainability.

Ethical Considerations:

Fair Competition:

Ensure that tactics used for entrapment or control do not involve unethical practices or create undue harm. Maintain fair competition and professional integrity in all actions.

Transparency:

While strategic manoeuvring may involve indirect approaches, it ensures transparency and honesty in stakeholder interactions and communications.

Long-Term Impact:

Consider the long-term implications of entrapment or control strategies. Ensure that such tactics contribute to positive outcomes and do not undermine relationships or industry reputation.

The strategy "Lure Your Enemy onto the Roof, Then Take Away the Ladder" emphasises entrapment and control to force opponents into vulnerable positions with limited options. Businesses can gain significant advantages in negotiations and competitive scenarios by strategically manoeuvring competitors or partners into disadvantageous positions. Balancing these tactics with ethical considerations and long-term goals ensures that strategies are effective, respectful, and sustainable.

Strategy 29: Tie Silk Blossoms to the Dead Tree

Core Concept: Illusion and Perception

The strategy "Tie Silk Blossoms to the Dead Tree" involves creating an illusion of vitality or value where there is none by enhancing the external appearance of something fundamentally lacking. This approach uses perception management to make something appear more attractive or valuable than it is, influencing how others perceive it.

Applications in Business and Competitive Positioning

1. Illusion and Perception

Managing illusion and perception in business involves creating a façade of success, capability, or appeal to influence stakeholders, customers, or competitors. This strategy can enhance brand appeal, attract investment, or influence market perceptions.

Example:

Marketing and Branding

A company might use sophisticated marketing techniques to enhance the perception of its products or services. For instance, a company could invest heavily in high-quality advertising, glamorous packaging, or celebrity endorsements to create an impression of high value or luxury, even if the product is relatively average. This strategy relies on appealing to consumer perceptions and emotions rather than the product's intrinsic qualities.

Example:

Corporate Image

A company might focus on creating a positive corporate image through public relations and community engagement efforts, even if its internal operations struggle. For example, a company might sponsor high-profile charitable events or engage in visible environmental sustainability initiatives to build a positive public image despite operational challenges or issues.

2. Brand Image and Market Positioning

Creating an illusion of value or success can be an effective strategy for brand image and market positioning. By enhancing the perceived value of a brand or product, businesses can differentiate themselves in the market and attract customer attention.

Example:

Luxury Branding

In the luxury market, brand image is crucial. A company might use exclusive store locations, limited-edition products, and high-end advertising to create an aura of exclusivity and desirability. Even if the products are not significantly different from competitors, the perceived luxury and prestige drive customer demand and premium pricing.

Example:

Product Launches

A company might create a sense of urgency and excitement during a product launch through limited-time offers, high-profile launch events, or strategic leaks. By generating hype and making the product seem like a must-have item, the company can attract attention and drive initial sales, even if the product's actual features or benefits are not revolutionary.

Fundamental Principles and Ethical Considerations

Key Principles:

Perception Management:

Focus on managing perceptions and creating favourable illusions to enhance brand image and market positioning. Ensure that the façade aligns with overall business objectives and strategic goals.

Strategic Presentation:

Use illusion and perception strategically to influence stakeholder perceptions, attract customers, and achieve competitive advantages.

Consistency:

Maintain consistency between perceived and actual value over time to build and sustain trust with customers and stakeholders.

Ethical Considerations:

Honesty and Transparency:

Avoid misleading or deceptive practices. Ensure that the illusion created does not involve false claims or misrepresentations that could harm stakeholders or lead to legal issues.

Customer Trust:

Consider the long-term impact of creating illusions on customer trust and loyalty. To avoid damaging the brand's reputation, ensure that the perceived value is supported by genuine quality and value.

Sustainability:

Evaluate the sustainability of using perception management strategies. Ensure that they contribute to long-term success and do not create short-term gains at the expense of long-term viability.

The strategy "Tie Silk Blossoms to the Dead Tree" emphasises illusion and perception to enhance the attractiveness or value of something that may not inherently possess those qualities. By strategically managing perceptions, businesses can influence market positioning, attract customers, and achieve competitive advantages. Balancing these tactics with ethical considerations and focusing on long-term value ensures that strategies are effective, respectful, and sustainable.

Strategy 30: Exchange the Role of Guest for That of Host

Core Concept: Role Reversal and Power Dynamics

The strategy "Exchange the Role of Guest for That of Host" involves shifting roles or positions to change a situation's power dynamics. By reversing roles, one can gain control, influence, or strategic advantage previously held by the other party. This approach helps manage power dynamics, control situations, and influence outcomes.

Applications in Business and Competitive Positioning

1. Role Reversal and Power Dynamics

In business, role reversal involves strategically shifting roles or responsibilities to gain control or influence. This tactic can be effective in negotiations, partnerships, and competitive scenarios where altering power dynamics can lead to favourable outcomes.

Example:

Strategic Partnerships

A company might initially approach a strategic partner or competitor as a subordinate or ally but gradually shift the dynamic by taking a leadership or controlling role. For instance, a smaller company might start by offering joint ventures or collaborations where it plays a supportive role. Over time, as the partnership develops, the smaller company could leverage its contributions or innovations to take a leading role, thus reversing the initial power dynamic.

Example:

Market Positioning

A company might position itself as a follower or secondary player in a market, only to later emerge as a leader or innovator. For instance, a business could initially adopt a low-profile strategy in a niche market, focusing on building expertise and relationships. As it gains credibility and market share, it can shift to a more prominent role, influencing market trends and setting new standards.

2. Hostile Takeovers and Negotiation Tactics

In hostile takeovers and negotiation scenarios, this strategy involves taking control of a situation by reversing roles or dynamics to gain leverage and achieve strategic goals. Changing the power dynamics can create acquisition, negotiation, or influence opportunities.

Example:

Hostile Takeover

In a hostile takeover, a company might strategically acquire a target company by initially presenting itself as a passive or supportive investor. Over time, the acquiring company could gain enough influence and control to take over the target company's board or operations. This role reversal shifts the power from the target company to the acquirer, enabling the takeover to be executed.

Example:

Negotiation Strategy

In high-stakes negotiations, one party might initially adopt a submissive or accommodating role to build rapport and gain trust. Once a foundation is established, the negotiating party can shift to a more assertive or controlling position, leveraging the established relationship to secure more favourable terms or concessions.

Fundamental Principles and Ethical Considerations

Key Principles:

Strategic Role Reversal:

Use role reversal strategically to manage power dynamics and gain control in negotiations or competitive situations. Ensure that the role shift aligns with overall objectives and long-term goals.

Leverage and Influence:

Employ role reversal to gain leverage and influence in negotiations, partnerships, or acquisitions. Be mindful of how shifting roles can impact relationships and outcomes.

Control and Balance:

Maintain control and balance throughout the role reversal process to ensure that the shift in power dynamics is managed effectively and aligns with strategic objectives.

Ethical Considerations:

Transparency and Fairness:

Ensure that role reversal strategies are implemented transparently and fairly. Avoid deceptive practices or manipulations that could undermine trust or lead to ethical concerns.

Respect and Integrity:

Maintain respect and integrity in interactions with stakeholders, competitors, and partners. Ensure that role reversal tactics do not harm relationships or create undue disadvantage.

Long-Term Impact:

Consider the long-term impact of role reversal strategies on organisational reputation, relationships, and sustainability. Ensure that tactics contribute to positive outcomes and do not create lasting negative consequences.

The "Exchange the Role of Guest for That of Host" strategy highlights role reversal to manage power dynamics, gain control, and influence outcomes. Businesses and individuals can achieve favourable results in negotiations, partnerships, and competitive scenarios by strategically shifting roles and positions. Balancing these tactics with ethical considerations and focusing on long-term goals ensures that strategies are effective, respectful, and sustainable.

Strategy 31: The Strategy of Beautiful Women

Core Concept: Strategic Attraction and Charm

"The Strategy of Beautiful Women" revolves around attracting, charming, or appealing to influence others and achieve strategic objectives. This approach involves leveraging aesthetic appeal or charismatic presence to gain favour, build relationships, and sway opinions or decisions.

Applications in Business and Competitive Positioning

1. Strategic Attraction and Charm

Strategic attraction and charm in business involve appealing, charismatic, or engaging presentations to influence stakeholders, customers, or partners. This can be applied through branding, marketing, or personal interactions to create positive impressions and facilitate desired outcomes.

Example:

Branding and Marketing

A company might use attractive design, compelling visuals, and engaging content to create a strong brand presence and appeal to target audiences. For instance, a luxury brand might focus on elegant advertising, high-end packaging, and a sophisticated brand image to attract affluent customers. By creating an appealing brand experience, the company enhances its market positioning and draws attention from its desired customer base.

Example:

Customer Engagement

Employees might use charm and personable interaction in customer service or sales to build client rapport and trust. For example, a salesperson might use a friendly demeanour, attentiveness, and personalised service to create a positive customer experience, increasing sales and customer loyalty. The strategic use of charm helps build lasting relationships and achieve business goals.

2. Influencing and Negotiation Techniques

In influencing and negotiation scenarios, leveraging strategic attraction and charm involves using personal appeal or persuasive techniques to sway opinions, secure agreements, or gain leverage. This approach focuses on creating favourable conditions through interpersonal influence.

Example:

Persuasive Negotiations

Charm and persuasive communication might influence the other party's negotiation decisions. For instance, a negotiator might employ engaging storytelling, positive reinforcement, and empathetic listening to build a strong rapport and gain the other party's trust. This strategic use of charm helps achieve favourable terms and build positive negotiation outcomes.

Example:

Influential Leadership

Leaders often use charm and strategic appeal to motivate and inspire their teams. For example, a leader might use charismatic speeches, personal stories, and visible enthusiasm to engage and energise employees. By effectively using charm and influence, the leader can foster a positive organisational culture and drive team performance.

Fundamental Principles and Ethical Considerations

Key Principles:

Authenticity:

Use charm and attraction authentically to build genuine relationships and influence. Ensure that interactions and strategies reflect true intentions and values.

Strategic Appeal:

Leverage charm and appeal strategically to achieve business objectives or negotiation goals. Focus on creating positive impressions and facilitating desired outcomes.

Relationship Building:

Use strategic attraction to build and strengthen relationships with stakeholders, customers, and partners, contributing to long-term success and collaboration.

Ethical Considerations:

Respect and Integrity:

Maintain respect and integrity in interactions, avoiding manipulative or deceptive practices. Ensure that charm and appeal are used ethically, not undermining trust or authenticity.

Transparency:

When using charm or strategic attraction, be transparent about intentions and objectives. Ensure that all parties involved understand the genuine motives behind interactions.

Long-Term Impact:

Consider the long-term impact of using charm and attraction strategies. Ensure that they contribute to positive relationships and sustainable success rather than creating short-term gains at the expense of long-term credibility.

"The Strategy of Beautiful Women" underscores strategic attraction and charm to influence and achieve objectives. Businesses and individuals can effectively enhance their market positioning, build strong relationships, and influence outcomes by leveraging appeal and charisma. Balancing these approaches with authenticity, respect, and ethical considerations ensures that strategies are effective, respectful, and conducive to long-term success.

Strategy 32: The Strategy of Open City Gates

Core Concept: Vulnerability as Strength

"The Strategy of Open City Gates" involves using apparent vulnerability or openness to create strategic advantages. By presenting oneself as accessible, transparent, or vulnerable, one can often disarm potential threats, build trust, and foster positive relationships. This approach leverages the perception of vulnerability to strengthen position and achieve strategic goals.

Applications in Business and Competitive Positioning

1. Vulnerability as Strength

In business, presenting openness or vulnerability can be a powerful tool for building trust and creating opportunities. By being transparent and approachable, companies can foster stronger relationships with customers, partners, and stakeholders.

Example:

Customer Relations

A company might openly address and acknowledge past mistakes or challenges. For example, if a company faced a product recall, it could transparently communicate the issue to customers, explain the steps taken to resolve it, and outline improvements made. This openness can enhance customer trust, demonstrate accountability, and ultimately strengthen customer loyalty.

Example:

Organisational Culture

Leaders might adopt an open and approachable style in organisational settings, openly discussing challenges and seeking employee input. This can create a culture of transparency and collaboration, making employees feel valued and engaged. Leaders can foster a more supportive and motivated team by openly acknowledging and addressing organisational weaknesses or challenges.

2. Openness and Transparency in Business

Embracing openness and transparency involves sharing information and being accessible to stakeholders, leading to increased trust, collaboration, and strategic advantages. This strategy can be particularly effective in negotiations, partnerships, and market positioning.

Example:

Transparent Communication

A company might adopt a transparent communication strategy, regularly sharing updates on business performance, strategic goals, and company initiatives. For instance, a publicly traded company could provide detailed reports on financial performance, strategic initiatives, and future outlooks. This transparency can enhance investor confidence, improve market perception, and build stronger stakeholder relationships.

Example:

Strategic Partnerships

In forming strategic partnerships, a company might openly share its goals, challenges, and expectations with potential partners. The company can attract like-minded partners aligned with its vision by being transparent about its needs and objectives. This openness can lead to more effective collaborations and mutually beneficial outcomes.

Fundamental Principles and Ethical Considerations

Key Principles:

Strategic Openness:

Use openness and transparency strategically to build trust, enhance relationships, and create opportunities. Ensure that the level of transparency aligns with overall business objectives and goals.

Building Trust:

Leverage vulnerability and transparency to build and strengthen trust with stakeholders, customers, and partners. Focus on creating authentic and positive interactions.

Strength in Vulnerability:

Recognise that presenting vulnerability can be a strength by demonstrating authenticity and accountability, leading to improved relationships and outcomes.

Ethical Considerations:

Authenticity:

Ensure that openness and transparency are genuine and reflect true intentions. Avoid using vulnerability as a deceptive tactic or for manipulative purposes.

Privacy and Confidentiality:

Balance transparency with protecting sensitive information. Ensure that openness does not compromise privacy or confidentiality.

Long-Term Impact:

Consider the long-term impact of adopting an open and transparent approach. Ensure that it contributes to sustainable trust and positive relationships rather than creating short-term gains at the expense of long-term credibility.

The strategy "The Strategy of Open City Gates" highlights the power of vulnerability and openness in achieving strategic objectives. By adopting a transparent and approachable stance, businesses can build trust, foster positive relationships, and create opportunities for growth and collaboration. Balancing these approaches with authenticity, privacy considerations, and a focus on long-term impact ensures that strategies are effective, respectful, and conducive to lasting success.

Strategy 33: The Strategy of Sowing Discord

Core Concept: Divide and Conquer

"The Strategy of Sowing Discord" involves creating or exacerbating divisions and conflicts within a group or between competitors to weaken their collective strength and achieve strategic advantages. One can disrupt cohesion and cooperation by fostering discord, making achieving goals and exerting influence easier.

Applications in Business and Competitive Positioning

1. Divide and Conquer

In business, dividing and conquering involves strategically creating or amplifying conflicts to weaken competitors or internal challenges. This approach can disrupt competitors, manage internal conflicts, or influence market dynamics.

Example:

Competitive Disruption

A company might use tactics to sow discord among competitors by publicly highlighting conflicts or discrepancies between them. For instance, a company could reveal information about disagreements or competitive weaknesses among rival firms, creating confusion and reducing their ability to present a united front. This can lead to decreased market effectiveness and provide a strategic advantage to the company employing these tactics.

Example:

Market Segmentation

In a highly competitive market, a business might create targeted marketing campaigns that emphasise the differences between its products and those of competitors. By highlighting perceived weaknesses or differences, the company can drive a wedge between competitor offerings and customer preferences, encouraging customers to switch brands and reducing the competitors' market share.

2. Internal and External Conflict Management

This strategy can also be applied to managing internal and external conflicts within an organisation or business environment. One can influence outcomes, shift dynamics, or achieve specific objectives by strategically managing or creating disputes.

Example:

Internal Team Dynamics

A leader or manager might strategically use internal conflicts to their advantage by addressing or highlighting issues that can lead to realignment or reorganisation. For example, suppose a team is struggling with collaboration. In that case, a leader might use specific conflicts to push for team structure or process changes, ultimately leading to more effective teamwork and improved performance.

Example:

External Stakeholder Relations

A company might manage external conflicts with stakeholders, such as suppliers or partners, by creating scenarios that reveal or exacerbate underlying issues. For example, by strategically addressing supplier disputes or public criticisms, a company can position itself more favourably, negotiate better terms, or gain leverage.

Fundamental Principles and Ethical Considerations

Key Principles:

Strategic Disruption:

Use discord strategically to weaken competitors or manage conflicts. Ensure that the approach aligns with overall business objectives and enhances strategic positioning.

Influencing Outcomes:

Leverage discord to influence outcomes, shift dynamics, or achieve specific goals. Focus on creating conditions that favour achieving strategic advantages.

Conflict Management:

Use Discord to manage conflicts within or outside the organisation and create positive changes or improvements.

Ethical Considerations:

Integrity and Respect:

Ensure that tactics used to sow discord are respectful and do not involve unethical practices or harm to individuals or organisations. Avoid creating unnecessary or malicious conflicts.

Transparency:

Maintain transparency and honesty in dealings with stakeholders, ensuring that conflict management strategies are communicated clearly and ethically.

Long-Term Impact:

Consider the long-term impact of using Discord as a strategy. Ensure that the approach contributes to sustainable success and does not undermine trust or relationships in the long term.

The strategy "The Strategy of Sowing Discord" underscores the use of division and conflict to weaken competitors or manage internal and external challenges. Businesses and individuals can influence outcomes, shift dynamics, and achieve strategic objectives by creating or exacerbating conflicts. Balancing these tactics with ethical considerations and focusing on long-term success ensures that strategies are effective, respectful, and conducive to lasting positive impact.

Strategy 34: The Strategy of Injuring Yourself

Core Concept: Sacrifice for Strategic Advantage

"The Strategy of Injuring Yourself" involves deliberately making a temporary sacrifice or creating a disadvantage to achieve a more significant strategic advantage. By incurring a short-term setback, one can create opportunities for long-term gains, deceive competitors, or influence outcomes in a favourable direction.

Applications in Business and Competitive Positioning

1. Sacrifice for Strategic Advantage

In business, this strategy involves making calculated sacrifices or facing temporary setbacks to gain a more significant advantage or achieve long-term objectives. This could include financial losses, reputation management, or temporary operational disruptions.

Example:

Loss Leader Pricing

A company might use loss leader pricing, selling a product at a loss to attract customers and drive traffic. Sacrificing short-term profit on the initial product can increase sales of higher-margin products and services. By creating a compelling offer, the company aims to build a customer base and achieve greater profitability in the long run.

Example:

Public Relations

Sometimes, a company might address and publicly apologise for a mistake or controversy, thereby accepting short-term reputational damage. This approach can help rebuild stakeholder trust, demonstrate accountability, and strengthen the brand's long-term position. The strategic sacrifice of reputation in the short term can lead to improved relationships and brand loyalty in the long run.

2. Risk Management and Competitive Strategy

Using strategically calculated risks or temporary disadvantages can effectively manage competitive dynamics and achieve business goals. This approach involves managing and mitigating risks while positioning oneself for future success.

Example:

Strategic Retreat

A company might intentionally scale back its operations or exit a market segment to focus on core competencies or more lucrative opportunities. This strategic retreat involves a temporary loss of market presence or revenue but allows the company to concentrate resources on areas with higher growth potential and competitive advantage.

Example:

Competitive Disruption

A company might deliberately undercut prices or accept lower margins in a highly competitive industry to disrupt competitors and capture market share. While this approach involves sacrificing immediate profitability, it can weaken competitors, attract customers, and create a stronger market position over time.

Fundamental Principles and Ethical Considerations

Key Principles:

Calculated Sacrifice:

Strategically make sacrifices or accept temporary setbacks, ensuring they align with overall business objectives and contribute to long-term gains.

Strategic Planning:

Plan and execute sacrifices with careful consideration of potential risks and rewards. Ensure that the strategy supports long-term goals and competitive positioning.

Risk Management:

Manage and mitigate risks associated with temporary sacrifices, ensuring they do not jeopardise overall business stability or reputation.

Ethical Considerations:

Transparency:

When making sacrifices or facing setbacks, be transparent about your intentions and strategies. Ensure that stakeholders understand the rationale and benefits of the approach.

Impact on Stakeholders:

Consider the implications of strategic sacrifices on employees, customers, and other stakeholders. Ensure that actions are respectful and do not unduly harm or disadvantage others.

Long-Term Sustainability:

Evaluate the strategy's long-term sustainability. Ensure that temporary sacrifices lead to genuine and sustainable advantages rather than short-term gains at the expense of long-term viability.

"The Strategy of Injuring Yourself" highlights deliberate sacrifices or setbacks to achieve more strategic advantages. By strategically managing and mitigating risks, businesses can create opportunities for long-term success, influence competitive dynamics, and position themselves for future growth. Balancing these tactics with careful planning, ethical considerations, and a focus on long-term goals ensures that strategies are effective, respectful, and conducive to lasting success.

Strategy 35: The Strategy of Combining Tactics

Core Concept: Synergy and Integrated Strategy

"The Strategy of Combining Tactics" involves integrating multiple tactical approaches to create a cohesive and synergistic overall strategy. Combining various tactics can leverage their collective strengths, enhance effectiveness, and achieve more significant outcomes than using any single tactic in isolation.

Applications in Business and Competitive Positioning

1. Synergy and Integrated Strategy

In business, combining tactics involves integrating various strategies and methods to create a unified and practical approach. This can enhance operational efficiency, improve market positioning, and achieve strategic goals more comprehensively.

Example:

Multi-Channel Marketing

To create a comprehensive marketing strategy, a company might use digital marketing, social media, traditional advertising, and public relations. By integrating these channels, the company ensures a broader reach, consistent messaging, and a more engaging customer experience. This synergy helps build brand awareness, generate leads, and increase sales.

Example:

Product Development

To develop a new product, a company might combine tactics such as customer feedback, competitive analysis, and market research. By integrating these approaches, the company can create a product that meets customer needs, stands out in the market, and responds effectively to competitive pressures. This integrated strategy leads to more innovative and successful product offerings.

2. Comprehensive Strategic Planning

Combining tactics involves strategic planning to ensure that various approaches are aligned and mutually reinforcing. This comprehensive planning helps optimise resource allocation, achieve strategic objectives, and address complex challenges.

Example:

Strategic Partnerships

A business might combine joint ventures, strategic alliances, and co-branding partnerships to expand its market presence and capabilities. By integrating these approaches, the company can leverage complementary strengths, access new markets, and enhance competitive positioning. This comprehensive strategy enables the company to achieve broader strategic goals and create value for stakeholders.

Example:

Risk Management

To address potential risks, a company might combine diversification, insurance, and contingency planning tactics in risk management. By integrating these approaches, the company can create a robust risk management strategy that mitigates various risks and ensures business continuity. This comprehensive approach helps manage uncertainties and achieve long-term stability.

Fundamental Principles and Ethical Considerations

Key Principles:

Integrated Approach:

Use an integrated approach to combine multiple tactics effectively. Ensure that various strategies are aligned and work together to achieve comprehensive goals.

Synergy and Efficiency:

Leverage the synergy created by combining tactics to enhance operational efficiency, market positioning, and strategic outcomes. Focus on creating value through integrated efforts.

Strategic Alignment:

Ensure all tactics and strategies align with overall business objectives and contribute to long-term success.

Ethical Considerations:

Transparency and Communication:

When integrating various tactics, maintain transparency and effective communication. Ensure that stakeholders understand the rationale and benefits of the combined approach.

Respect for Stakeholders:

Consider the impact of integrated tactics on stakeholders, including employees, customers, and partners. Ensure that combined strategies respect their interests and contributions.

Sustainability and Long-Term Impact:

Evaluate the sustainability and long-term impact of combining tactics. Ensure that integrated strategies lead to lasting benefits and do not create short-term gains at the expense of long-term viability.

"The Strategy of Combining Tactics" emphasises integrating multiple approaches to create a unified and effective strategy. By leveraging synergy and comprehensive planning, businesses can enhance their operational efficiency, market positioning, and overall strategic success. Balancing these tactics with strategic alignment, transparency, and ethical considerations ensures that integrated strategies are effective, respectful, and conducive to long-term achievements.

Strategy 36: If All Else Fails, Retreat

Core Concept: Strategic Withdrawal and Preservation

The "If All Else Fails, Retreat" strategy involves strategically withdrawing or retreating from a challenging situation to preserve resources, regroup, and reassess. This approach emphasises the importance of knowing when to step back to avoid unnecessary losses and create opportunities for future success.

Applications in Business and Competitive Positioning

1. Strategic Withdrawal and Preservation

In business, strategic withdrawal involves scaling back or exiting from a market, project, or initiative when it becomes clear that continuing would result in significant losses or failure to achieve desired outcomes. This approach helps preserve resources and maintain long-term viability.

Example:

Market Exit

A company might exit a market facing insurmountable competition or declining demand. By withdrawing from the market, the company can focus its resources on more profitable opportunities and avoid further financial losses. This strategic retreat allows the company to preserve capital and redirect efforts toward areas with better growth potential.

Example:

Project Termination

When a project consistently underperforms or faces insurmountable obstacles, a company might terminate it rather than continue investing time and resources. This decision helps minimise losses and reallocate resources to more promising initiatives. The strategic withdrawal enables the company to focus on areas with higher chances of success and growth.

2. Crisis Management and Strategic Pivots

Making a strategic retreat or pivot involves reassessing the situation, managing risks, and adapting strategies to navigate challenges effectively in crises. This approach helps manage crises, protect core assets, and set the stage for future recovery and success.

Example:

Crisis Management

During a financial downturn or economic crisis, a company might implement cost-cutting measures, such as reducing overhead, scaling back operations, or temporarily halting expansion plans. These actions represent a strategic retreat to manage financial risks and preserve liquidity. By focusing on core operations and essential functions, the company can navigate the crisis and position itself for future recovery.

Example:

Strategic Pivot

A company facing significant challenges in its primary business model might decide to pivot to a new market or product line. For example, a technology company struggling with declining hardware sales might shift focus to software or digital services. This strategic pivot involves temporarily withdrawing from the original business model while reallocating resources and efforts to new opportunities. The pivot allows the company to adapt to changing market conditions and explore new growth avenues.

Fundamental Principles and Ethical Considerations

Key Principles:

Strategic Assessment:

Assess situations regularly to determine when a strategic withdrawal or retreat is necessary. Ensure that decisions are based on a thorough evaluation of risks, opportunities, and overall objectives.

Resource Preservation:

When making a strategic retreat, focus on preserving financial, human, and operational resources. This approach helps maintain long-term viability and sets the stage for future success.

Adaptation and Flexibility:

Respond adaptably and flexiblely to changing circumstances. Use strategic retreats to reassess, pivot, and realign strategies with evolving conditions.

Ethical Considerations:

Transparency and Communication:

Communicate transparently with stakeholders about the reasons for strategic withdrawals or pivots. Ensure that all parties are informed and understand the rationale behind decisions.

Impact on Stakeholders:

Consider the implications of strategic retreats on employees, customers, partners, and other stakeholders. Ensure that actions are taken with respect and consideration for their interests and well-being.

Long-Term Vision:

Maintain a long-term vision and focus on sustainable success. Ensure that strategic retreats or pivots contribute to overall business resilience and growth rather than short-term gains at the expense of future viability.

The "If All Else Fails, Retreat" strategy underscores the importance of strategic withdrawal and adaptation in challenging situations. Businesses can effectively manage crises, mitigate risks, and set the stage for future success by making informed decisions to step back, preserve resources, and pivot when necessary. Balancing these tactics with strategic assessment, transparency, and ethical considerations ensures that retreats and pivots are conducted respectfully and contribute to long-term achievements.

Conclusion

Mastering strategic thinking is crucial for navigating the complex landscape of modern life and business. This book outlines 36 strategies that offer timeless wisdom on approaching various situations with strategic insight and adaptability. By synthesising these strategies, we can better understand their practical applications and how they can be effectively employed in contemporary contexts.

Synthesising the 36 Strategies

The 36 Strategies provide a diverse toolkit for tackling different scenarios, each offering unique insights into strategic thinking and problem-solving. While the strategies vary in focus— from deception and misdirection to sacrifice and adaptation—they collectively emphasise a common theme:

The importance of flexibility, foresight, and tactical understanding.

By synthesising these strategies, we recognise that effective strategy is not rigid adherence to one approach but integrating various tactics to address specific challenges. For instance:

Deception and Misdirection:

Tactics like "Fool the Emperor to Cross the Sea" and "Clamour in the East, Attack in the West" teach the value of misdirection and create strategic confusion.

Sacrifice and Strategic Retreat:

Strategies such as "Sacrifice the Plum Tree in Place of the Peach" and "If All Else Fails, Retreat" highlight the importance of making calculated sacrifices for more significant long-term gains.

Integration and Adaptation:

Approaches like "The Strategy of Combining Tactics" and "The Strategy of Open City Gates" demonstrate the power of integrating various methods and adaptability in changing circumstances.

Practical Applications in Modern Contexts

Applying these strategies in contemporary settings requires an understanding of modern dynamics and an ability to adapt traditional wisdom to current realities. Here's how some key strategies can be applied today:

Strategic Misdirection:

In business negotiations or competitive markets, tactics like "Hide Your Dagger Behind a Smile" and "Clamour in the East, Attack in the West" can gain leverage and outmanoeuvre competitors through clever positioning and misdirection.

Innovation and Adaptation:

Strategies such as "Create Something from Nothing" and "Shed Your Skin Like the Golden Cicada" are particularly relevant in an era of rapid technological change and market disruption. Companies that innovate and adapt are better positioned to thrive in dynamic environments.

Crisis Management:

Tactics like "Loot a Burning House" and "If All Else Fails, Retreat" offer valuable insights for managing crises and making strategic withdrawals to preserve resources and focus on recovery.

These strategies can inform individuals' decision-making, career management, and conflict resolution. Understanding when to adapt, innovate, or strategically withdraw can lead to more effective personal and professional outcomes.

Final Thoughts on Strategic Mastery

Strategic mastery is not about adhering to a single doctrine but cultivating a versatile and adaptive mindset. The 36 Strategies provide a framework for thinking strategically, but their true power lies in their application. Mastery comes from understanding the underlying principles of each strategy and using them to navigate the complexities of modern life and business.

Practical strategists are those who can:

Integrate Multiple Approaches:

Combine various strategies to create a comprehensive and adaptable approach tailored to specific challenges.

Embrace Flexibility:

Recognise the need for flexibility and adaptability and be prepared to pivot as circumstances evolve.

Maintain Ethical Integrity:

Apply strategies with respect for others and a focus on long-term success, ensuring that tactical decisions are made with ethical considerations.

By synthesising the wisdom of these 36 Strategies and applying them thoughtfully, individuals and organisations can enhance their strategic thinking, navigate challenges more effectively, and achieve their goals with greater confidence and success.

References

For those interested in further exploring the concepts of strategy and tactics, a wide array of resources—from classic texts to contemporary analyses—can provide additional insights and perspectives. Here's a curated list of further reading and resources to deepen your understanding of strategic thinking and its applications:

Books on Strategy and Tactics

"The Art of War" by Sun Tzu

A foundational text on strategy and military tactics that has influenced various fields beyond warfare, including business and leadership.

Sun-tzu, Minford, J. (2008) *The Art of War*. 1st ed. Penguin Classics.

"The Book of Five Rings" by Miyamoto Musashi

A classic work on strategy, tactics, and martial arts by a renowned samurai, offering insights into combat strategy and mental discipline.

Musashi, M. (2012) *The Book of Five Rings*. Shambhala Publications Inc.

"Strategy: A History" by Lawrence Freedman

A comprehensive overview of strategic thought from ancient times to the present, exploring how strategy has evolved and its application in various contexts.

Freedman, L. (2015) *Strategy:*

A History. 2nd ed. Oxford University Press.

"Good Strategy Bad Strategy: The Difference and Why It Matters" by Richard Rumelt

An exploration of what constitutes effective strategy and how to avoid common pitfalls in strategic planning.

Rumelt, R. (2012) *Good Strategy Bad Strategy:*

The Difference and Why it Matters. Main ed. Profile Books Ltd.

"The 48 Laws of Power" by Robert Greene

Based on historical examples and psychological principles, it is a provocative and insightful examination of power dynamics, strategy, and influence.

Greene, R., Elffers, J. (1999) *The 48 Laws of Power*. 1st ed. Penguin.

"Thinking, Fast and Slow" by Daniel Kahneman

While not solely focused on strategy, this book offers valuable insights into decision-making processes and cognitive biases that impact strategic thinking.

Kahneman, D. (2012) *Thinking, Fast and Slow*. 1st ed. Penguin.

"The Lean Startup: How Today's Entrepreneurs Use Continuous Innovation to Create Radically Successful Businesses" by Eric Ries

A modern approach to strategy and innovation in the startup world, emphasising iterative development and adaptation.

Ries, E. (2011) *The Lean Startup:*

How Today's Entrepreneurs Use Continuous Innovation to Create Radically Successful Businesses. Crown Publishing Group, Division of Random House Inc.

"The Art of Strategy: A Game Theorist's Guide to Success in Business and Life" by Avinash K. Dixit and Barry J. Nalebuff

An accessible introduction to game theory and its applications in strategic decision-making.

Dixit, A. K., Nalebuff, B. J. (2010) *The Art of Strategy:*

A Game Theorist's Guide to Success in Business and Life. W. W. Norton & Company.

"24 Laws of Life: Timeless Wisdom for a Meaningful Life" by B Archer

a transformative guide that blends ancient wisdom with contemporary relevance.

Archer, B. (2024) *The 24 Laws of Life:*

Timeless wisdom for a meaningful life. Independently published.

Articles and Journals

"Harvard Business Review"

Top business thinkers and practitioners offer a wealth of articles on strategic management, innovation, and leadership.

"Strategic Management Journal"

A leading academic journal that publishes research on strategic management theory and practice.

"Journal of Strategic and International Studies"

Provides analysis and insights into strategic issues on an international scale, including policy, security, and global strategy.

Online Resources and Websites

Harvard Business Review Online (hbr.org)

Features articles, case studies, strategy, leadership, and management insights.

Strategy+Business (strategy-business.com)

A publication from PwC that offers articles and insights on strategy, management, and business trends.

MIT Sloan Management Review (sloanreview.mit.edu)

Provides research-based articles on business strategy, innovation, and technology.

The Art of War: A Visual Guide (artofwarvisualguide.com)

An online resource that offers visual summaries and interpretations of Sun Tzu's "The Art of War."

Coursera and edX

Platforms offering online courses on strategic management, business strategy, and related topics from leading universities and institutions.

Videos and Lectures

TED Talks

Features numerous talks on strategy, leadership, and decision-making by experts and thought leaders.

YouTube Channels

Channels like "CrashCourse" and "The School of Life" offer accessible content on strategy and business concepts.

Khan Academy

Provides educational videos on economics, business, and strategic thinking.

Professional Organisations and Networks

Strategic Management Society (strategicmanagement.net)

A professional organisation focused on advancing the field of strategic management through conferences, publications, and networking opportunities.

American Management Association (amanet.org)

Offers resources, training, and certification in management, strategy, and leadership.

Institute for Strategy and Competitiveness (isc.hbs.edu)

A research institute at Harvard Business School dedicated to advancing knowledge in strategy and competitive advantage.

By exploring these resources, readers can better understand strategic principles, contemporary applications, and the evolving landscape of strategy and tactics.

www.ingramcontent.com/pod-product-compliance
Lightning Source LLC
Chambersburg PA
CBHW031926240526
45464CB00023B/1722